RADICAL RENEWAL
OF GLOBAL SOCIETY

Radical Renewal of Global Society

Nursultan Nazarbayev

translated by Richard Samuel

STACEY
INTERNATIONAL

STACEY INTERNATIONAL

128 Kensington Church Street

London W8 4BH

Tel: +44 (0)20 7221 7166; Fax: +44 (0)20 7792 9288

Email: info@stacey-international.co.uk

www.stacey-international.co.uk

ISBN: 978-1-906768-39-3

CIP Data: A catalogue record for this book is available from the British Library

Contents

List of diagrams

A time for global strategic decisions

The waves of global crisis which have swept across our planet since the beginning of the present millennium should prompt us to reflect ever more deeply on the fate which the whole of mankind now shares. It is becoming clearer than ever how far the development of world society and the local communities within it are interconnected and interdependent, and how important it is to combine the efforts of countries and peoples in the search for mutual survival, well-being and prosperity.

Among the most pressing and topical problems mankind is facing are the following:

Firstly, the energy and ecological crisis, which has thrown into doubt the scope for balancing programmes for energy security against the needs of environmental protection;

Secondly, the global crisis in food supplies, despite the agricultural successes achieved in a number of countries, which has resulted in hunger for hundreds of millions of the world's inhabitants, particularly in Africa, and in starvation for thousands of them;

Thirdly, the existing pattern of economic relationships has led to a sharp polarization in income levels, to a widening gap between a small number of rich countries, the so-called 'golden billion', and the majority of poor countries which lack the resources they must have if they are to modernize their economies and provide a decent living standard for their people.

The crises the world is facing are by no means confined to these particular problems. The financial crisis which erupted in 2007 demonstrated beyond doubt that the monetary and financial systems devoted to maximum profits and to speculation in the money markets had led to the creation of virtual capital divorced from the real economy, with the bursting of bubbles which damaged the lives of many millions of people. It should be noted also that current levels of scientific development, education and cultural institution correspond neither with the realities of the new historical period in which we live, nor with the tasks we face in development and innovation. Radical renewal of our social and cultural institutions is vital.

Thus it becomes clear that the entire system of relationships in our global society must face up to profound upheavals and challenges requiring systemic solutions. I regard this as the most important task confronting the United Nations, as the only institution with a comprehensive global reach and the ability both to establish dialogue and partnership between countries and to overcome the crises we face in the new century. When I addressed the UN General Assembly on 25 September 2007 I proposed that a global strategy for energy and ecological development should be created, which could then be discussed at a World Summit on Stable Development in 2012 in the heart of the Eurasian continent, in the Kazakh capital Astana, which possesses all the necessary facilities for this task.

It now seems to me necessary to go further, and to take account of the vast changes resulting from the global crises and the lessons we must learn from them. What is needed is a discussion which goes beyond energy resources and ecological challenges, to address a strategy for tackling global problems as a whole. It should provide a coherent answer to the challenges of our new century, from energy and the environment to the problems of the overall human dimension, such as social and demographic challenges, technology and innovation, and economic, geopolitical, socio-cultural issues. To put it another way, what we need is a systematic approach to the transformation and radical renewal of all aspects of life in our global community. Achieving this, furthermore, will be possible only if we can unite our efforts and establish partnerships across the whole range of the issues that world society demands.

I have given my support to an initiative undertaken by Russian and Kazakh scholars in this respect. They have embarked on the complicated and responsible task of working out a long-term forecast of the stage civilization may have reached by the middle of the twenty-first century. As a basis for such a global forecast, they have proposed a methodology for integrated long-term forecasting, combining the teachings of Nikolai Kondratyev and Joseph Schumpeter on cycles, crises and innovation; the theory of civilizations and socio-cultural dynamics by Pitirim Sorokin, Arnold Toynbee, Ferdinand Braudel; the noosphere theory by Vladimir Vernadski and Nikita Moiseyev, and the balance-based method for long-term economic forecasting of the Nobel Laureate Vasili Leontiyev and other researchers.

In dealing with future developments on both the global and local levels the concentration should, in my view, be on the basic realities likely to be uppermost in the years immediately ahead of us. The long-term forecasts, based on the work of the Russian and Kazakh researchers I have mentioned, can be presented to the United Nations and used as a basis for a long-term global strategy for implementation through dialogue and partnership between the nations involved. The underlying aim of the present study is to provide a first draft of proposals for a strategy of radical renewal within the global community. This could then be discussed at the World Summit.

If the response to this initiative is positive we should be able, within a relatively short period, to work out a scientifically researched and dependable programme of action for the global community as a whole. This could lead, within two to three decades, to a purposeful transformation for the first time in world history, aimed at bringing about a post-industrial civilization which incorporates the aspirations and interests of the bulk of the world's population.

The twenty-first century that we are now entering is a period which will see a deepening of integration between the various communities on this planet and intensification of their dialogue and partnership, in order to resolve the new range of problems confronting mankind as a whole. I think we can be confident in saying that the contemporary world at the beginning of the twenty-first century is one of local societies which display the extensive variety of our historical inheritance and the contemporary life of the communities which constitute them. It is only by preserving and developing this variety within the framework of partnerships that societies can hope to flourish in the future, and make possible the avoidance both of conflict between them and of the threat posed by accumulated stockpiles of weapons. A characteristic feature of the early twenty-first century is the multipolar nature of relations between states, set in a global context. Trends within global societies which effectively bring together the interests and individual destinies of mankind are becoming more apparent, as ties between peoples and nation states become closer: they cannot exclude any one country or field of human endeavour.

The structure of civilized societies reflects the multidimensional limits within which their dynamics and variety can largely be appreciated, including the local variants in our present-day communities. This is the factor which defines the vitality of the megasystem which mankind constitutes within our global civilization.

CHAPTER 1

Outline strategy for a radical renewal of global partnerships

1.1   From dialogue to partnership between civilizations

Over the millennia, conflicts in human society have existed side by side with many different kinds of dialogue, involving mutually advantageous exchanges of ideas, technologies, and trade in goods. For centuries what one might call highroads for dialogue and exchanges have been developed between different cultures: the Silk and Tea Routes across the territory of what is now Kazakhstan, the Volga river route, and, among others, the land links between the Greeks and Varangians. Such trade routes were given protection by the states which used them and gave rise to the establishment of dozens of towns and centres for trade and the creation of manufactured goods. It is by no means accidental that Russia and Kazakhstan are currently in active discussion about the creation of a new canal, the 'Eurasia', to connect the Caspian and the Black Seas by the shortest possible route.

Dialogue and partnership embrace many different areas in the lives of the societies involved. These are in part spiritual and intellectual: the sciences, cultural activities, education, religion; also mutually beneficial exchanges in goods and services; the spread of new technologies and information systems, construction materials, energy supplies and economic inputs into the organization of production. In addition, they are promoted by a variety of political factors, the work of democratic institutions and the workings of the legal system on the everyday life of individuals in society. The significance of this was clearly recognised internationally at the turn of the twenty-first century when the United Nations declared 2001, as the first year of the new century, to be the year of dialogue between the world's communities.[1] It was in November 2001 that the General Assembly adopted a resolution entitled 'Global agenda for dialogue between civilizations' which set out a plan of action to that effect for states, international organizations and non-governmental agencies. The resolution noted that 'all civilizations celebrate the unity and multifaceted nature of mankind, are enriched and further developed by dialogue between them' and that 'it is essential to acknowledge and respect the richness of all civilizations and to seek the common factors which unite them, in order to find comprehensive solutions to all the problems which mankind must confront.' The dialogue between civilizations on the basis of equality and mutual respect is only the first step towards cooperation in the world community. The highest form of cooperation is partnership between civilizations in resolving global problems, which is the foundation of the multipolar nature of world society in the twenty-first century. It is important to note that dialogue and partnership are inseparably interconnected. Without such dialogue and mutual comprehension partnership is impossible, as is the attainment of united efforts in resolving common problems. Awareness is growing that the future lies with multipolarity, based on dialogue and partnership, as a response to the global challenges of the twenty-first century.

1.2 The fundamental contradictions and challenges to civilization in the twenty-first century

Differing interests and conflicts in world society are inevitable. They spring from historical legacies, from the difficulty of bringing about transformation in contemporary conditions, and from the polarization of economic, technological and social development. When such conflicts become acute, as they do from time to time, what is important is not to impose solutions, but for both sides to seek mutual understanding and compromise, the principle being to give priority to the processes of integration and development, while respecting local interests.

Our world has accumulated a mass of conflicts of interest and huge problems on a global scale which demand partnership between individual countries and larger groupings for their solution. Such are the struggle against international terrorism, the threats of global warming and worldwide epidemics, the backwardness of many societies and the search for energy security. There are, indeed, generally acknowledged international institutions through which partnerships can be established to overcome these, such as the UN, the OSCE, the Shanghai Cooperation Organisation and many other international bodies and organizations. Kazakhstan is active in all of these and has proposed a range of initiatives to develop their work further. The work of Russian and Kazakh scholars has shown how the origin of global crises at the start of the present millennium is to be found in two sets of technological challenges. In the first place, the potential for industrial and technological production is nearing exhaustion as the productivity growth rate and economic dynamism slow down. In the second place, the technological gulf between developed and developing countries is widening in a way which condemns the more backward countries, in which most of the human population lives, to technological and economic decline, because of their inability to cope with complex new challenges. The industrialization of production which began in the technical revolutions at the end of the eighteenth and beginning of the nineteenth centuries gave the leading countries involved huge impetus, with sometimes tenfold increases, to their productive capacity; this enabled them to lower their production costs and to establish market dominance throughout the world. However, by the end of the twentieth century it became apparent that the potential of the industrial epoch had been virtually exhausted, and that technical progress was no longer providing the anticipated high rates of productivity growth and the economic dynamism which accompanies it. The global economy as a whole faced serious tensions, as the rate of population growth remained high and most countries suffered serious shortages of the resources they needed to cope with their growing economic and social problems.

Inequities in the monetary and financial systems across the world have created a burdensome and profound technological crisis which will evidently continue to afflict the whole of the first quarter of the twenty-first century. Resolving it will in turn require new post-industrial technologies and new and more equitable monetary and financial arrangements. The legacy of two hundred years of industrial development of the traditional type has led to deep polarization between the states which make up the global community. This has led to a sharp break in levels of productivity between advanced and more backward countries, dividing the world between the 'golden billion' and several billion who continue to live with poverty and deprivation.

In 2006, for example, World Bank statistics show that gross domestic product per head in the 'golden billion', with a population of 1,031 million inhabitants was 56 times higher than that of low-income populations totalling some 2,420 million, while labour productivity was 13 times higher. A breakthrough in securing improved levels of innovation in the poorer countries will, therefore, require, above all, much closer interaction between them and the richest, since otherwise they will be quite unable to acquire the new and much more effective technologies that are essential for their development.

These problems are exacerbated by the activities of transnational corporations that exploit their technological supremacy in their pursuit of maximum profits and benefit from exports of high technology to countries with medium or low capacities in this respect. Many of these corporations inflate prices or artificially slow price reductions in relation to their production costs in order to fortify their new technological stranglehold. Narrowing this gap will call for the adoption of new approaches on a worldwide basis, a global technological strategy mounted by the United Nations and put into effect by its subordinate bodies such as the UN Development Programme.

Such programmes must entail systematic and substantial assistance with the spread and adoption of the latest technologies to the less technologically advanced and lowest income countries. The advanced societies, particularly in North America, Western Europe and Japan, are at present devoting enormous resources towards achieving breakthroughs in the assimilation of the new sixth stage technologies. For this purpose they possess all the necessary technological, human and financial resources, while the majority of other countries face serious challenges to which they are in no position to respond appropriately. Furthermore, a number of rapidly developing countries such as China, India, Russia, Brazil and some others are in a position both to achieve breakthrough in some relatively limited areas and establish competitive levels of production in them. The lack of adequate resources will, however, deny this possibility to many countries in Africa and Asia. As a consequence, the technological gap which had opened up towards the beginning of the twenty-first century has only got wider. And it is likely to become wider still as the leading economies adopt sixth stage technologies, while the less advanced remain in the lower stages.

This deepening gulf between rich and poor countries might even prove to be the sort of powder keg which could blow up the world community itself. This is why it should be a global priority to raise technological standards and promote innovation on a planetary scale, the objective being to ensure that the fruits of the technological revolution in the present century are enjoyed not just by the restricted circle of countries of the 'golden billion' but by all societies and nations on our planet. This will call for a large-scale transfer of current and potential technologies from the leading countries to the less advanced, thus creating an effective mechanism for partnership on a planetary scale.

It is a historical fact that a fundamental characteristic of the current technological revolution has been the creation of new generations of armaments and highly accurate weaponry. This has provoked a new spiral in the arms race, as has been seen in many countries during the past century. Such a revolution in military technology unquestionably threatens the whole of mankind with annihilation through the creation and employment of new types of weapons of mass destruction. What is needed, therefore, is a completely new direction in the politics of technology, to ensure that our best intellectual efforts and resources are put not into weapons of destruction and self-destruction but into overcoming the technological crisis which has gripped the world at the start of the twenty-first century.

A systemic change of this kind is a task for academics, politicians and public and private leaders across the international community. Its guiding principles should be those of partnerships capable of taking on the challenges and threats of the new millennium; it should also work to a timescale which would be adequate to bring about a radical renewal of society on a global scale and be capable of dealing with the broad trends of our new historical era.

1.3   Strategies for a breakthrough in global innovation

This strategy should, in the first place, be conceived in such a way as to bring about the fundamental innovations which are at the core of the scientific and technological revolution taking place in the first years of the twenty-first century. For this, all countries and societies must unite their efforts. I share the view of Simon Kuznets, Nobel prizewinner in economics, a view amplified by the Russian economist Yuri Yakovets, that alongside a huge number of useful innovations and a relatively small number of basic new innovations which have provided the foundations of new generations of technology, there are truly epoch-making discoveries. These appear only at rare intervals and, when they do, take technology on to fundamentally new stages. Epoch-making innovations are to be found in the transitional stages of new technology-driven production processes, and it is precisely now that we face the necessity for such innovations, as well as the relatively less momentous ones, to be given support by state authorities and by global society as a whole and the relevant international organisations.

One such innovative mechanism is the renewal of the whole monetary and financial system, which must be put at the service of innovations in the world's productive processes. This can be done through the recently created mechanism for global partnership: the G20, though detailed implementation must be carried out through the United Nations and other organizations, including the major regional groupings. The fourth chapter of the present book will discuss this issue in greater detail. It must be for the UN, the UN Development Programme and other international organizations to support the introduction of the first and second order innovations already referred to which constitute the core of the scientific and technological revolution in the first half of the twenty-first century; also the dissemination of sixth stage technology, as a first step in creating the post-industrial technological production system. Unless state authorities and international organisations provide such support, the breakthrough in global technology will be very slow in coming and is likely to be accompanied by increased polarization between one country or society and another. The results of the work done at the sixth stage of technology are beginning to emerge in advanced societies with the accelerated development of nanotechnologies, to which substantial resources have been allocated. These hold great promise both for the development of new and promising generations of physical materials and for many solutions to new problems affecting the lives and activities of mankind as a whole. The understanding and evolution of new types of alternative and renewable sources of energy should be another area benefitting from this research. There are still further areas and directions to be identified which will facilitate the transformation of technology in society, so as to speed up productivity growth and that of the economy more generally.

Both government agencies and the leading corporations in advanced countries are concentrating their efforts on incorporating the basic innovations of the sixth stage of technology into their economies, calculating that combining this with substantial other resources will increase their international competitiveness and help them to overcome the economic and other problems they currently face.

In the second place, innovation must have a human face: it must take place within a social context, with the overriding aim of raising the level of human potential. It is people who have to bring about breakthroughs in innovation, make new discoveries and bring such inventions to the point where they bring practical benefit to their societies. Joseph Schumpeter was absolutely right to point to the importance of the entrepreneur both as an innovator and as the initiator of improved productive capacity by the application of new scientific ideas. But it is also for the leaders of individual governments and international institutions to evolve strategies for securing breakthroughs in innovation. In giving technological progress a human dimension a vital role will be played by ensuring that the education of young people fosters a spirit of innovation, starting at the school and student level, with experience of actual production and of the work of government services. Similar considerations should be applied to projects in the fields of medicine and public health. The objective here should be to prevent the spread of epidemics, to speed up understanding of their causes, to raise health standards and improve mortality rates from infancy onwards, and to promote longer and healthier lives. This becomes increasingly important as global populations include ever larger proportions of the elderly. Innovative approaches should also be used to improve living and employment conditions for millions of workers throughout the planet by freeing them from the burdens of heavy and boringly repetitious labour, in favour of a more creative and active way of life. At their St Petersburg summit in July 2006 the G8 focussed on the role of education in bringing about such innovative breakthroughs.

In the third place, any breakthroughs in technological progress must depend on the extent to which ecological and wider spiritual and intellectual dimensions can be brought to bear on them. Changes in the character of scientific and technical progress must also be subject to a fuller and more effective approach to the use of natural resources, including processing with zero or minimal contamination by waste products and drastic reduction of harmful emissions into the environment. At the same time, the increasingly substantial replacement of natural resources by alternative sources of energy and materials should make possible reductions in the use of irreplaceable minerals and satisfy society's needs accordingly. By doing this we should be able to take fuller account of the needs of future generations, as well as our own, by preserving unrenewable mineral resources, forests, water supplies and productive farmland.

In the fourth place, the globalization of scientific and technological progress directly affects revolutionary innovation itself. The fact is that the scale of the technological transformation the planet is experiencing makes it impossible for even the most powerful society to secure precedence over all others. Progress in achieving innovation through interconnected technological links requires a division of functions between individual countries and mutually supporting systems capable of bringing about such progress, the raising of standards and cooperation and integration on a global scale. This is why it is so important to establish better divisions of labour and other forms of cooperation to achieve the sixth stage of technology on a worldwide basis.

In the fifth place, the technological innovations needed for a global strategy in the twenty-first century demand that we find ways of bridging the chasm that separates the most advanced and more backward societies on our planet.

1.4   Partnership in the sociological and cultural sphere

The principles of partnership should extend to all the most important areas in our various societies, whether we are speaking of the sciences, education, cultural activities or systems of religious belief. Of these, particular priority should be accorded to the sciences, with the aim of establishing a knowledge-based society, to facilitate a solid basis for innovative renewal and enhanced productive capacity, whose technological achievements can be made accessible to global society as a whole. The member countries of the Commonwealth of Independent States, which form the core of civilization in the Eurasian landmass, that is to say Russia, Kazakhstan, Ukraine and Belarus, possess an enormous scientific potential. This should be made more active use of, by incorporating into their activities the best specialists and experts, including youthful talent as well, whose partnership will in turn facilitate social progress throughout the world. Other scholars from a number of countries are well known in this area, such as Francois Guizot and Thomas Bockel, Nikolai Danilevski and Oswald Spengler, Arnold Toynbee and Pitirim Sorokin, to whom I have earlier referred. However, such distinguished scholars face the task not only of studying the theory and history of past civilizations, but of seeking to forecast their future trajectories. The world community, in the shape of the leading international organizations such as the UN, UNESCO and others should thus seek to establish a long-term strategy by engaging in dialogue and partnership with a view to forecasting the 'Future of Civilization' for the period up to the middle of the twenty-first century. In this connection the preparation of the UN's long-term global forecast 'Energy and Ecological Strategy up to 2050' takes on a particular significance (see Chapter 2).

Partnership in the field of education has a vital role, in that it determines the quality of people's potential and capacity for productive labour. Low-income countries have significant numbers of illiterates, especially among the female population, and consequently are very short of workers capable of mastering current technologies; this is a major factor in causing technical and economic backwardness. There are also in the global population hundreds of millions of illiterates who are 15 years of age or older. It was natural for this problem to figure in the discussion of the G8 in St Petersburg in July 2006, and it led to the adoption of a document entitled 'Education for innovative societies in the twenty-first Century' which noted the basic landmarks in the development of the three topics 'education, science and innovation', the reconstruction of the educational process, including the adoption of present-day information technologies to promote innovation, and the need to combat illiteracy in backward countries. I consider that an important aspect of partnership in the field of education must depend on forecasts of requirements in elementary, intermediate and higher education so as to establish what present-day priorities should be.

UNESCO is working on an international programme 'Education for All' in the period up to 2015, designed to meet United Nations educational objectives, and it is expected that countries which possess considerable potential in that area should take an active part in it. They will need to ensure up-to-date content for the educational programmes and internet sites to meet twenty-first century requirements, for which UNESCO assistance would be useful.

I am deeply convinced that in our own country the achievement of a national policy will require an effective programme for the development of Kazakh language and culture. For me, it is of great importance that our society has in recent years come to realise the fundamental role in our society of the Kazakh language and culture as a way of building a policy of tolerance and friendship between our peoples. As before, we shall continue to support the use of Russian in our society as a means of integrating our country into the wider international community. We must also understand that modernization will require knowledge of English and other foreign languages. Another important issue for our rising generation will be the acquisition of comprehensive and reliable knowledge of the history of other civilizations and the dialogue and partnership between them. The example we should follow here is that of the legendary Muslim ruler Sultan az-Zakhir Beibaris, an acclaimed son of the Kazakh people and an outstanding ruler of Egypt and Syria in the thirteenth century, who symbolizes our country's historical and cultural unity. He halted the Mongol invasions of the Muslim East and Christian West and defeated the crusaders in the Middle East, and was remarkable for his concern for and protection of developments in science, education, art and architecture. Awareness of such achievements, which are to be encountered elsewhere in the history of world civilization, should also inspire our present-day politicians and leading figures in society and religious culture. Equally complex are the cultural challenges, since they entail the preservation of cultural variety, the legacy of global and national cultures, and the development of dialogue and mutual interaction between different traditions. In November 2001 the UNESCO General Conference adopted a Declaration on Cultural Diversity, which defined culture in broad terms as the combination in a society or social group of distinguishing features, whether spiritual, material, intellectual or emotional.[2]

As well as art and literature, culture embraces ways of life, value systems, the ability to share one's community with others, traditions and spiritual beliefs. The Declaration stresses that respect for cultural diversity, tolerance, dialogue and cooperation, trust and mutual understanding is the best guarantee of peace and international security. The processes of globalization with the rapid growth in information and communications technologies present a challenge to such cultural diversity, while creating new conditions for dialogue between different societies. We need to take account both of the possibilities and conflicts which can arise from the rapid spread of the global internet and telecommunications networks.

On the one hand they create opportunities for hundreds of millions of people, especially of the younger generation, to gain rapid access to the information they require. On the other, the information obtainable through the internet is designed to disseminate western values, is filled with scenes of violence, and encourages people to forget their own national and cultural identities.

For its part, Kazakhstan has a rich multinational culture and is taking steps to preserve its cultural diversity and the internal dialogue that goes with it. One of the measures we have taken to achieve this has been a series with two component parts: 'Cultural inheritance' was a government programme which was presented over the period 2004 to 2006, with a second programme covering the period 2007 to 2009, which is in progress at present. Together they have confirmed the features common to the cultures of both Europe and Asia. This positive outcome has encouraged me to ask for a project to be worked out for a further national programme to be known as 'Cultural inheritance' for the period 2009 to 2011. While the first two programmes were devoted to the demonstration, discovery, accumulation and study of the enormous cultural inheritance of Asia and Europe, the next national programme will be devoted to presenting this as the property of the whole of our society. One of the most important constituents of the system of social and cultural values is religion, and its role in our society. Its insights express the ideals and aspirations of believers and create the conditions for norms of behaviour to develop. At the heart of the world religions are the moral norms of tolerance and mutual understanding, the strength of family ties, the seal of non-violence and openness to other faiths.

At the same time, we find that religious intolerance, fanaticism and extremism do from time to time provoke clashes between cultures, violent conflict, the rejection of persons of different persuasions and xenophobia. During recent decades it has been noticeable that two conflicting tendencies have emerged in the spiritual life of society, against the background of a renaissance of individual world religions and a strengthening of their roles, both nationally and internationally. One tendency encourages mutual understanding and dialogue between the different faiths, seeks to find common ground on basic world issues and promotes respect towards persons of different faith, or none. The other seeks to promote religious fanaticism and extremism among some sections of the faithful, supports international terrorism under the banner of struggle against the unbelievers, and strives to establish nation states on the basis of religion. This second tendency is extremely dangerous and has provoked opposition in global society and its political and intellectual elites.

Kazakhstan is a secular multinational state; the constitutional foundations of our state embrace freedom of conscience, respect for all religions and systems of belief, and a rejection of extremist views, regardless of their religious affiliation. We have devoted considerable efforts to encouraging interfaith dialogue. We have already held three congresses with leaders of world and traditional religions, a forum for foreign ministers from Muslim and western countries, under the title of 'Our common world: progress through diversity'. Kazakhstan has also presented an initiative to the United Nations proposing that 2010 be declared a year in which cultures and religions can be brought closer together.

At the sixtieth session of the General Assembly of the UN two resolutions were adopted: 'On the encouragement of interfaith dialogue and cooperation in the name of peace' and 'Encouragement of religious and cultural understanding, harmony and cooperation'. These documents emphasize the importance of mutual understanding, tolerance and friendship in the whole diversity of their religions, convictions, cultures and languages. They note that tolerance in relation to cultural, linguistic, ethnic and religious diversity and dialogue between different societies are indispensable conditions for peace, mutual understanding and friendship between countries and peoples.

1.5   Institutions and mechanisms for global partnership

The current processes of transformation can be carried out successfully, provided they are based on adequate institutions and processes which are functioning adequately. The most widely recognised institution in this respect is the United Nations with its offshoots: the Economic and Social Council, UNESCO, UNDP, UNEP and others. The General Assembly, the Security Council and the UN Secretary General have played a decisive role in settling many international conflicts and in working out proposals for stable development and ecological security, as well as in humanitarian cooperation. Indeed, the UN is the main forum for dialogue and cooperation in the world community. Even it, however, is not immune from defects. Cooperation is also increasing between the financial and economic institutions such as the International Monetary Fund, the World Bank, the International Trade Organisation and others, though they suffer from the fact that they have not as yet fully established the principle of partnership across the whole of global society. Institutions for this purpose are emerging in bodies such as the Asian-Pacific Economic Cooperation Organisation, the Shanghai Cooperation Organisation, the OSCE, the Conference on Cooperation and Confidence-building in Asia and others. They are well placed to set up regional centres for integration and partnerships and to resolve local conflicts.

Kazakhstan is playing an active part in the work of a number of global and regional partnership institutions, and is ready to promote their activities on the basis of multipolar peacemaking to the benefit of all mankind. A particularly important role among the international institutions is that of the G8, which brings together the leaders of most of the world's leading countries. They are responsible together for 49% of global exports, 51% of industrial production and hold 49% of the assets of the IMF. The G8 is an extremely important mechanism for economic and political coordination between the most developed countries. G8 summits act as a focus for discussion of the most pressing problems of concern to millions of people across the planet. Its role is not, however, confined to the economic and security-related potential of the participating countries; it is concerned also with the constructive task of resolving the most topical issues of the time, as these emerge at the yearly leaders' meetings. The political influence of the G8 members is such that the decisions they take provide in part a global vision which can guide societies worldwide and assume a universal character within the global institutions. Thus, the G8 has become one of the key institutions in the informal handling of political problems worldwide. It is, furthermore, one of the centres in which concepts for the management of international relations can be worked out: the basis for the so-called New World Order.

An increasingly significant role in the management of economic issues is the new body known as the G20. In this grouping, leaders of the main developed and developing countries unite their efforts to overcome global challenges like the financial crisis, to reach an understanding of its causes and, in order to prevent any recurrence, to agree on general rules for reforming the institutional and administrative mechanisms underlying the world's financial markets. The G20 is an informal economic association which takes in the European Union and 19 leading developed and developing countries, which include Argentina, Australia, Brazil, Canada, China, France, Germany, India, Indonesia, Italy, Japan, Mexico, Russia, Saudi Arabia, South Korea, Turkey, UAR, the United Kingdom and the United States. Their combined populations amount to two thirds of the world's total and they produce 85% of the world's gross national product. When I attended an economic summit in Boai, China, I proposed the establishment of an Asian equivalent, the A20, to address similar tasks in our continent and come forward with recommendations to overcome our Asian challenges. All the institutions I have mentioned can and should contribute to strengthening the democratization of international relations, to aim for fair solutions to existing global problems, and to the development of partnerships throughout the globe.

An analysis of contemporary problems reveals three particular ones which need to be addressed urgently: energy and ecological issues, technological issues and financial and economic problems. These are all interconnected and each reinforces the importance of the others: to deal with one without tackling the others is out of the question. The chapters which now follow will be devoted to examining possible ways of resolving these three groups of issues; my hope is that it will be possible to establish a strategy and work towards innovative solutions through dialogue and partnership within the international community.

CHAPTER 2

Strategy for energy
and ecological partnerships

At the beginning of the twenty-first century the world community encountered a new kind of threat: a global crisis with energy and food supplies, and with ecological problems which reinforced one another and threw into doubt the prospects for stable development across the board. At the present time, the most serious problems for the planet are the deepening energy crisis and the increasing dangers caused by unfavourable climate change. Radical and innovative solutions will depend on a clear understanding by the global community of the prospects for energy supplies and the ecological challenges involved. This is because energy supplies, like the environment as a whole, affect all parts of our planet; they thus present the most pressing economic and geopolitical problems which need to be resolved if the well-being of individual countries and the world community is to be safeguarded for the future.

Most specialists would agree that the world in the first half of the twenty-first century will be marked by colossal upheavals throughout its whole extent. The crisis in energy supplies and ecological challenges will demand an innovative and knowledge-based response and a corresponding approach to the problems of production and consumption. This will require a clear understanding of the best way to tackle global crises on a comprehensive basis, and the adoption by an innovative and well-informed society of an optimistic and groundbreaking approach to resolving them. It will fall to politicians, governments, academics and businessmen, and to the world community more generally, to develop scientifically based and long-term strategies to bring this about. Certain elements of the best strategic approach to a global programme for dealing with energy and ecological problems are beginning to emerge.

2.1 The energy and ecological dynamic: lessons of the crisis and basics of a strategy

The underlying causes of the global crisis over energy supplies and the environment can, in my view, be summed up as follows. The first is the gap between supply and demand. This can be seen in the growing discrepancy between growing demand and the limited availability of the traditional sources of energy from excavated resources. According to some estimates, world energy use from 1900 to 2000 expanded almost fifteen times, and will increase by a further 60–70% between 2000 and 2030. Similarly, the remaining supplies of oil and natural gas will now last for less than one hundred years. If current trends are maintained, yearly oil consumption will reach 3 billion tons by the year 2018. Even on the assumption that industrial-quality reserves increase substantially as a result of new discoveries, geologists calculate that by 2030 to 2040 80% of all global resources will have been exhausted. A factor to be taken into account is that with the extraction of the richest and most accessible reserves the cost and prices of what remains will continue to increase.

A further significant negative factor is that with present-day extraction techniques for hydrocarbon deposits, particularly of oil, considerably less than 100% can be exploited. A considerable proportion of the resources involved is also lost completely. While coal reserves are much greater than those of oil and natural gas, they are also not unlimited. Three quarters of global resources, amounting to approximately 10 trillion tons, are concentrated in the United States, the People's Republic of China and countries of the former USSR. In the 1990s world consumption amounted to 2.3 billion tons per annum. Consumption expanded considerably in developing as well as in the most highly industrialized countries.

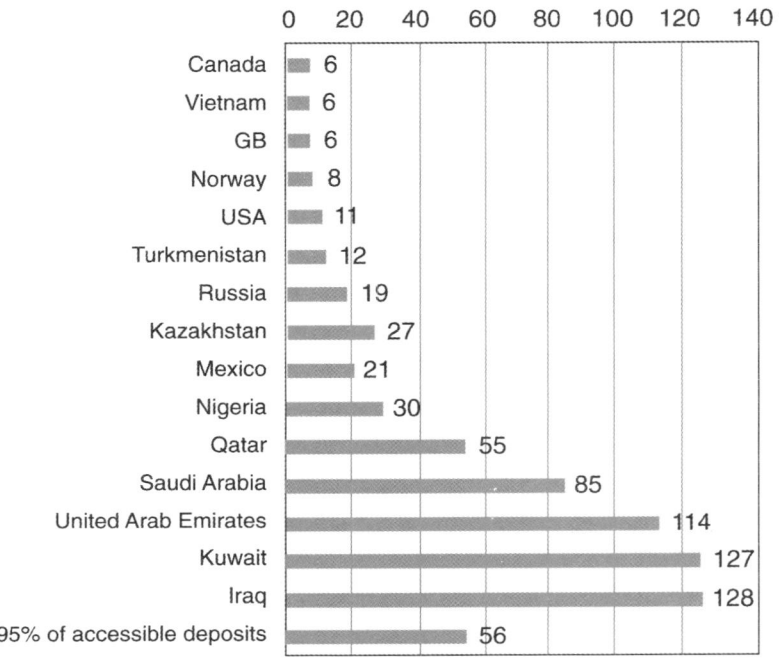

Diagram No 1: **Timeframe for extraction of known oil reserves in prime oil-producing countries**

According to current estimates, coal consumption maintained at the present level should last for 420 years; but if it increases significantly this could be reduced to not even as much as 200 years. Expanded use could, however, lead to increased emissions into the atmosphere of greenhouse gases. Since the G8 summit in Japan in 2008 agreed to a twofold reduction in greenhouse gas emissions by the year 2050, this may lead to decreasing use overall.

There are at least three factors connected with the increasing demand for energy resources. One of these relates to demography. The global trend is towards population increase, and, in consequence, expanded energy use per capita in low-income countries. The UN's medium calculation of demographic increase by 2050 is 47% and from 60% – 160% in less developed countries. The second factor is intensive economic development in such countries as China, India, Brazil, Malaysia and Middle Eastern states. It is estimated that their primary energy requirements will increase by 53% compared to the beginning of this century, while those of developing countries such as India and China will increase by 70%. The third factor is inefficient use of resources, particularly the wastefulness in energy use of industrial technologies and of current lifestyles.

The limited scope for satisfying the growing demand for energy resources is due to at least two further factors. First of all there is a disproportion between supplies of fossil fuel and its use in energy generation. Oil and gas make up less than a quarter of global supplies, but they provide over 80% of energy production. Coal and natural uranium, with 76% delivered, provide only 13% of energy supplies. Oil combustion, which makes up about 40% of total world energy consumption and oil products used as transport fuel, as well as for heat generation and electrical energy, produces up to 40% of atmospheric pollution. The second factor is the finite supply of excavated mineral resources for use in energy production. The world population is making increasingly intensive use of traditional mineral resources: oil, gas, coal and uranium and other minerals are being used to up to 85% of the world's energy requirements. While the experts may disagree on the timeframe (average timeframes for uninterrupted supplies of oil are 40 years; uranium: 50 years; gas: 60 years; coal: just over 150 years), they are all agreed that hydrocarbon fuel supplies will not last for ever.

Financial and economic factors are of great importance in establishing the causes of the energy and ecological crisis. If demand begins to exceed current rates of extraction, the price of oil will once again rise sharply and be followed a global fall in production, and economic crisis will follow. Looking at the problem from an economic perspective, the extraction, transportation and processing of hydrocarbons, which are located in remote and inaccessible regions of the planet, will become increasingly expensive and require growing investment. Morgan Stanley has calculated that the cost of geological exploration and of working new deposits has more than doubled since the beginning of this century. Oil-producing countries outside OPEC are planning to invest more than one trillion dollars on scientific research into perfecting technology for oil recovery and processing; this will have to be paid for. And while the profitability of using hydrocarbons in energy generation is still relatively high, the tendency for it to diminish is relatively obvious.

Turning to the geopolitical factors in the energy and ecological crisis, it should be noted that hydrocarbon deposits are extremely unevenly distributed from the geographical point of view, which leads to the topic of energy dependence. As a concept it has both a global and at the same time a relative dimension. It is global in the sense that it affects any given country irrespective of whether or it possesses natural energy resources or not. It is relative in the sense that any energy resources provide a competitive advantage which is nevertheless temporary. The truth of the matter is that two thirds of the planet's oil supplies are located in the Middle East, a region which is also all too well endowed with political crises and armed conflicts. Most specialists agree that the growing demand for oil in the future can only be satisfied by increasing deliveries from that source. And it should be noted that a drop in oil supplies of only 10–15% is enough to bring paralysis to the economies of the advanced industrial states. In the 1970s a reduction in oil production of only 5% led to more than a fourfold increase in prices. In such a situation the use of armed force to gain control of oil resources is already seen as a matter of both national and international security. This can then lead to geopolitical disputes and armed conflicts for control of promising hydrocarbon deposits, including under the world's oceans.

Whether we like it or not, oil and gas are becoming of great geopolitical importance, an effective lever for political manipulation, and a matter for energy-related blackmail, threats and terrorism. The sources and supply routes for energy resources are a potential and vulnerable target for attacks by international terrorists. It is as if we have crossed a frontier behind which until recently we could control our oil supplies: now they control us! We are prepared to pay an ever-increasing price for it, in both the practical and metaphorical senses of that word.

The natural world and the human population are no longer able to withstand the ecological damage being done to them as a result of irrational exploitation of hydrocarbons for energy supply. Thus we are already confronted by energy-related catastrophe. Every year traditional energy plants of various types are burning more than three billion tons of oil. Forty-five to fifty billion tons of air are consumed in this process and for every single person on earth up to 300 kilograms of noxious and even actively dangerous substances are spewed into the atmosphere. There is a scientific consensus that this is one of the main causes of the greenhouse effect, which heats up the atmosphere and leads to damaging climate change.

Up to 40% of the harmful emissions into the atmosphere are caused by the burning of oil and oil products to produce electricity and energy for heating. The World Health Organisation has noted that 30% of childhood illnesses are caused by ecological contamination, and around three million persons are killed every year by poisonous emissions into the atmosphere. The United Nations calculates that damage from global warming will cost mankind USD1 trillion every year by 2040. It was for this reason that the Kyoto conference in December 1997 adopted its document to reduce harmful emissions into the atmosphere. The characteristic symptoms of energy-related and ecological crisis began to emerge to a greater or lesser extent from the 1970s onwards and established themselves worldwide to the point where their effects are likely to become even more extreme in the twenty-first century.

In that connection I should like to stress that although the energy and ecological crisis is linked to the economic crisis, it has a number of distinguishing features of it own. The clearest connection was to be observed in 2008 when the sharp rise in energy prices, particularly for oil, made the production of manufactured goods more expensive and increased transportation costs; the result was a widespread reduction in manufacturing volumes which exacerbated the growing crisis in the financial institutions.

We might briefly sum up the problems in the following way. In the first place the economic crisis is illustrated by the decline in the basic macro-economic indicators, such as contraction in the rate of growth or demand for goods and services on the global market, the drop in gross domestic product and the like. At the same time, the crisis in the energy and ecological situation worldwide is marked by the growth in the extraction and consumption of primary energy resources and the increase in demand in the world energy market. This can be observed in the excess of supply over demand: the energy and ecological crisis can be seen in the fact that the demand for energy resources exceeds the available supply. In the second place, the economic crisis is accompanied by a decrease in emissions into the environment as a consequence of reduced production in resource-rich sectors, since the crisis shows up the opposite tendency: an increase in environmental pollution as a result of the use of mineral fuels. In the third place, the excess of supply over demand leads to falling prices on world markets and in the national markets of countries in the throes of economic crisis. In conditions of energy and ecological crisis, on the other hand, the excess of demand over supply brings about increases in world and domestic prices for energy carriers, after which the chain of price rises spreads to the whole economy, with a resulting wave of inflation. The coincidence over time of the economic and energy and ecological crises leads to the phenomenon that has come to be known as stagflation. I hope that things will not come to that point if we can understand correctly the forces at work and evolve a global strategy to deal with it.

The global energy and ecological 'imperative' was first formulated at the end of the last century by the Russian academic Nikita Moiseyev, who was one of the pioneers in the theory of the 'noosphere'. 'What we need,' wrote Moiseyev 'is to find a form of development capable of reconciling our needs and day-to-day activities with what the planet's biosphere can cope with, while allowing for future development. This is the most widely applicable statement of the imperative, in the sense that to breach it is to threaten mankind with degradation.'[3] The imperative, as it applies to energy and the ecology of the planet, is a call from the future to respond to an awareness of what is needed to develop the world's energy resources. Taking into account all these factors and the causes of the crisis I have described, I think it fair to say that the principal features of this development over the next 25 years are likely to be:

1) The preponderance of organic fuels as the main source of electrical and thermal energy; currently the proportions of organic minerals available for energy generation are as follows: coal 63.3%, natural gas 13.3% and oil 12.5%, while uranium provides 10.7%;

2) The growth in demand for primary fuel resources resulting from intensive economic development in certain countries and rapid population growth on a global scale;

3) The expansion of global and regional energy markets and the growing dependence of most countries on energy imports;

4) The increasing cost of hydrocarbon fuels, with the resulting rise in electrical energy and heating tariffs;

5) Moves to make economies less dependent on energy supplies, including conservation;

6) Improvements in hydrocarbon processing technologies to make them more efficient sources of energy;

7) Moves towards increased use of self-standing decentralized energy sources in the context of global electricity generation.

It can be expected that the relationships between energy suppliers will experience considerable changes as they change their behaviour in response to circumstances. The unpredictability of such changes may well cause instabilities both in specific markets and in the way the global economy itself develops. This is to look ahead only as far as 25 years. What is likely to happen next?

If we assume that total current trends in increased energy consumption per head of population are maintained up to the year 2050, there is no escaping the conclusion that we shall reach crisis point both over energy supplies and levels of harmful emissions released into the atmosphere. So we must ask ourselves what we can do today to help our descendants to avoid this fate. In recent times, many expert studies have been carried out on the influence of ecological factors on social and economic development both now and into the future. The United Nations Environment Programme has prepared a report on the 'Perspectives for the global environment' (GEO-4), which provides an extensive forecast of environmental changes globally and by individual region. It covers an extremely varied range of indicators beginning with basic factual data over the period from 2000 to 2050 examined on the basis of four possible scenarios.[4]

The first of these, 'Markets first', assumes that the private sector, with the active support of governments, achieves economic growth while adopting the best approach to preserving the environment and human welfare. It must be very doubtful that the private sector would, in fact, play such a leading role in tackling global problems of this kind. It was the private sector which must be held responsible for the great depression of the 30s; what is more, it provoked the current monetary and financial crisis, with all the damage that has done to the global system.

The second scenario, 'Policy first' assumes that it would be for governments to launch and see through firm policies for environmental improvement and human development, actively assisted by the private and social sectors. The 'leading and guiding' role of parties and politicians has too often diverted such efforts into the realm of no more than good intentions.

The third scenario, 'Security first', proposes that governments and the private sector should somehow compete for control of efforts to improve or sustain public well-being with the support of the richest and strongest elements in society. The assumption here seems to be that access to basic resources would be given to those with the most power and money. In practice, the outcome in this case would prove to be little different from the market approach.

The point of departure for the fourth scenario, 'Sustainability first', is close cooperation between civil society and the private sector to improve the environment and human well-being, with particular emphasis on fairness. In this case, equal weight would be given to environmental protection and to social and economic policy in conditions marked by transparency and legitimacy in the actions undertaken. Civil society has not developed in all countries of the globe, and similarly not all countries possess a sufficiently powerful private sector.

I conclude that the best approach would be to adopt the best elements from the second and fourth scenarios. For Kazakhstan and other developing countries a more realistic scenario for strategic development would be to combine:

1) Rapid progress towards high economic levels by intensifying the transition towards an innovatory type of development with support from both the government and the private sectors;

2) New technologies to manage production and the requirements of daily life with reduced demands on resources and the environment, working in collaboration with other countries.

If we are to help in tackling the ecological challenges which the whole world now faces we cannot get away this time from the need to study the experience gained in the 'highly developed West'. Only by understanding the connection between our national interests and our productive capacity and potential in science and technology will we in our country be in a position to contribute our own ideas to development in the rest of the world. Kazakhstan already has the opportunity of using the advantages it possesses through the extent of its territory and natural resources to develop a development strategy which will benefit both its own natural interests and the new global imperatives in the natural world, the economy and society as a whole. But to achieve this requires that human potential be established as the highest priority, with the emphasis on improving our education system and comprehensive support for science and invention.

One thing is very clear. We must not delay adopting measures to tackle the energy supply and ecological challenges that face us; we must constantly strive for new approaches to improve our existing technologies; this means that we must make our consumption more efficient, preserve natural and energy resources, and work on techniques for renewable energy and alternative sources. Even on the best projections we shall not be able to resolve the energy and ecological problems indefinitely. It is quite possible that by 2050 new applications of existing technology will allow us to overcome some of the most acute current difficulties. But the demands of the energy and ecological problems we face are too serious for us to be able to ignore them. Hence the need for the new technologies which we will consider below. For the moment we should note that, like every country to a greater or lesser extent, we shall inevitably run up against energy shortages, if we are not doing so already. This already imperils one of the most important elements in the development of a particular economy: productivity growth, without which economic growth is bound to decline. For this reason, conservation of energy and other resources must be priorities, along with the discovery and harnessing of new renewable resources and joint efforts on a global scale to secure energy security. These are topics to which I have already devoted many of my previous researches. There are three possible solutions to this basic problem:

1) Innovative development of existing energy technologies;

2) Innovation in renewable and alternative energy supplies;

3) Completely new technologies.

2.2 A global energy and ecological strategy: aims and approaches

An overall aim for a global energy and ecological strategy might be formulated as follows:

'The establishment of partnerships on a global scale to achieve, by the middle of the twenty-first century, the best possible allocation of energy and other natural resources between all communities and countries. This should be made possible by conservation of energy resources for the benefit of future generations, the twofold reduction of greenhouse emissions and other environmental contaminants, and the establishment of scrupulously planned programmes for production and consumption with all the necessary intellectual and ecological inputs.'

This general objective is to be brought about by means of the following interconnected elements:

The final aim must be to establish energy production and consumption on the foregoing principles. The point of departure is the formulation and implementation of a long-term energy and ecological strategy with partnerships on a global scale. The intermediate result would be a twofold reduction by the year 2050 of greenhouse gases and other atmospheric contaminants.

The intermediate and final objectives would require the following steps to be taken:

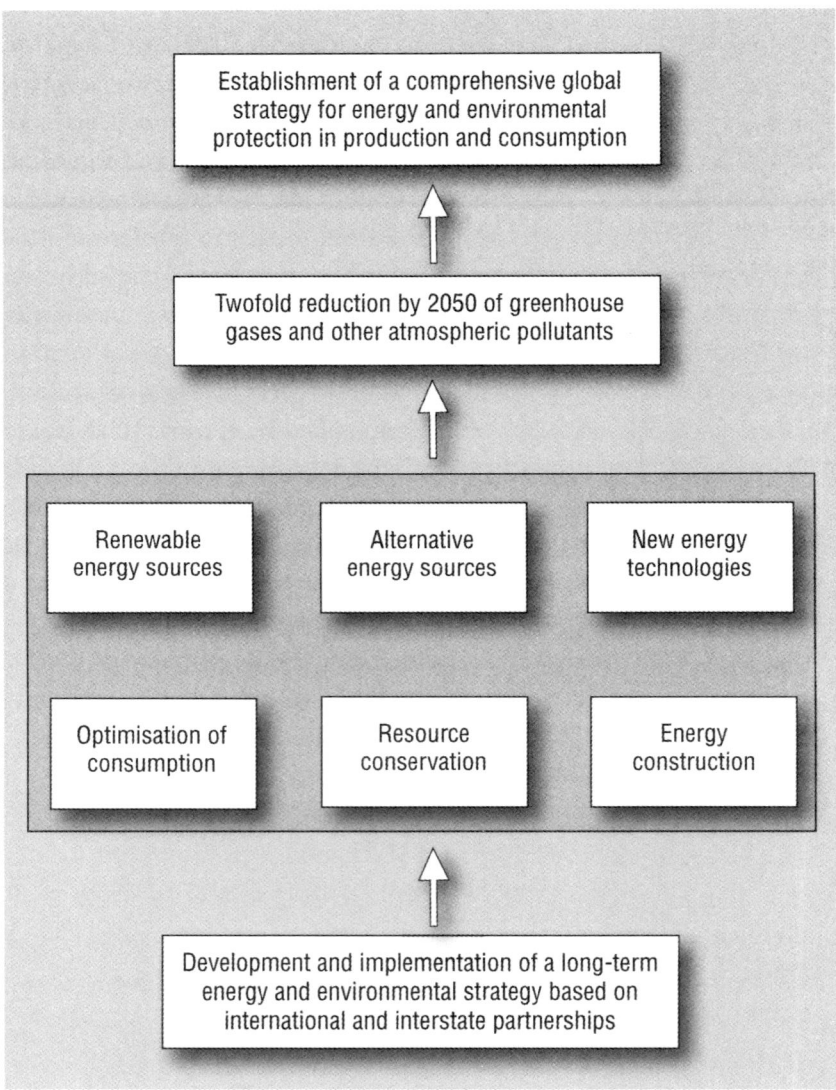

Diagram 2: **Objectives of a global strategy for energy and the environment**

1) Optimisation of consumption;
2) Conservation of resources;
3) Energy saving;
4) Renewable energy;
5) Alternative energy sources;
6) The necessity for new energy sources.

The successful completion of these steps will make possible the final aim of the strategy, which is to establish a soundly based means of production and consumption. We should now take a closer look at the significance and prospects for each of the above steps.

OPTIMISATION OF CONSUMPTION HAS TWO ASPECTS

1) Wasteful energy consumption by industrial enterprises and private individuals, which leads to the exhaustion of unrenewable resources and excessive environmental pollution;

2) Excessive disparities in levels of consumption in different individual countries and societies.

Dealing with the first of these issues must begin with an analysis of consumption patterns, followed by a scheme for distributing global resources across time and by geographical location. This distribution should take into account the requirements of each country against the background of its physical characteristics and climate, its technological capacities, its economic and social circumstances, energy and ecological requirements, patterns of food consumption and the lifestyle of the population. The next requirement will be the establishment of norms for consumption by each individual country within the global framework. This approach will make it easier to overcome discrepancies in the consumption of basic resources between one country and another. It will also clearly demand, in addition to the technological, economic and political inputs, an ethical and social dimension which takes accounts of global needs, extending down to those of the individual family. The difficulties of achieving such a distribution are all too evident. It will not be possible without radical changes in life styles and consumption patterns, as previously established earlier in the period of industrialization, which brought us to the dangerous crises of the second half of the twentieth century.

CONSERVATION OF NATURAL RESOURCES

Whatever progress may be made in science and technology, economic development is inseparable from ever-increasing consumption of natural resources. Of the more than 185 billion tons of coal and 45–50 billion tons of iron ore that have been extracted in the past 100 years, for example, over a half were mined between 1960 and 2000, a period of particularly intensive technological development. Consumption of other types of minerals, especially non-ferrous, required for alloy manufacture increased over that same period by 3 to 5 times and more, and raw materials for fertilizer by a factor of 3 to 3.5. The United States, China and Russia come first, second and third respectively in their consumption of mineral resources, which amounts to around 41% of the world total. In the next 50 years petroleum consumption is expected to increase 2 to 2.2 times; natural gas 3 to 3.2 times, iron ore 1.4 to 1.6 times, prime grade aluminium 1.5 to 2 times, copper 1.5 to1.7 times, nickel 2.6 to 2.8 times, zinc 1.2 to 1.4 times and other types of raw minerals 2.2 to 3.5 times.

Equally rapid is the demand for fresh water, and in some regions access to it is one of the most pressing problems of the twenty-first century. One third of the world's population lives in countries already experiencing some or significant water shortages. The World Bank calculates that in the first quarter of the present century this proportion may rise to a half or more of the world population without institutional reforms to improve the conservation and distribution of water resources. In these new circumstances there can hardly fail to be conflicts on a global scale for control of natural resources. One can hardly describe as satisfactory the work that is being done to introduce ecological standards, norms for more effective consumption of resources, and restrictions on uncontrolled waste disposal. Restrictions cannot resolve the problem or make its solution more evident since they are not directed at restraining those who are transferring the lion's share of prime resource consumption to developing countries, who are then obliged to adopt 'dirty' productive methods which do most to poison the natural environment.

If developing countries are to approach the technological levels highly developed countries have reached in conserving resources, the former have no alternative but to improve their technical capacities by substantial capital investment. Other ways of dealing with the problems of natural resources will have to be found.

How can we overcome the contradiction between the requirements of further economic growth and the maximum ecological demands that can be placed on the natural world? The conservation of natural resources must in the first place be brought about by innovations in our economic management. For developing countries, including Kazakhstan itself, this can only happen if their economies take a new and innovative direction. This must be done, first and foremost, by taking due account of the negative consequences that have flowed from the globalization of the world's mineral and raw material resources:

1) The majority of developed industrial countries are gradually squeezing out enterprises on their territories which have been extracting and processing raw mineral resources in favour of imports;

2) The world market in almost all types of raw mineral resources is at present saturated; producers in industrial countries which are in a position to influence their countries' trade policies have no interest in new sellers who may offer products at low prices;

3) Excessive increases in exports of fuel and energy resources and of basic liquid metals from CIS countries have reduced raw

material supplies for their own national industries and restricted their ability to function effectively;

4) CIS exports of strategic and critically important types of raw mineral resources have not been accompanied by effective use of their foreign exchange receipts in the industrial sector.

The social and economic situation of CIS countries has come to depend increasingly on prices imposed by the world markets and to be influenced by discrimination against companies active in these countries. To put it another way, globalization is placing the world's resources in the hands of the 'First World' and creating divisions between one part of the world's population and the others. The only way to deal with this is to create partnerships of global reach in technology and innovation. I shall deal with this in greater detail in the next chapter of the present book. For the moment I will mention only the importance of developing countries having their economies raised to the level of the sixth technological stage, in which an active feature must be the employment of new types of energy policy, and at the same time, a transition to the production of less energy-intensive products and new materials derived from the fruits of research into nanotechnology, biotechnology and the like.

Kazakhstan embarked on that path when we adopted our 'Strategy for industrial and innovative development for the period 2003 to 2015'. Kazakhstan's need for such innovatory policies in conserving our natural resources derives from the fact that we lag well behind the United States and other advanced countries in our adoption of energy security. Energy consumption per head in Kazakhstan is 4320 kilowatt hours (kWh), which is 3.3 times lower than the United States. In the highly developed countries overall the consumption of electrical energy per head is around 9000 kWh. Kazakhstan also lags behind the USA and Western Europe in its GNP in proportion to every unit of electrical energy. Each unit we make (for 1 kilogram of oil equivalent) generates USD 1.9 compared to USD5.3 in the European Union. The seriousness of our economy's shortcomings in energy production is all too clear, and with it the importance of driving through a programme of transition to a more innovative approach. This is something that we must do today: we must heed the expert forecasts that 'catastrophe may strike us by the middle of the twenty-first century and so quickly that it may be too late to take any remedial measures to prevent it.'[3]

It follows that dealing with the preservation of natural resources will require unconventional thinking and a creative approach to forging new forms of cooperation across national boundaries. This is particularly true for conservation efforts, which must be acceptable to the mainstream of international opinion.

Another aspect of this will be how best to agree on rational use of existing natural resources, and to achieve worldwide conservation for the benefit of future generations. Extraction and exploitation of energy and other mineral resources, the felling of forests (the green lungs of the planet) contraction of arable land and consumption of fresh water are proceeding at a pace which means we are in effect living off credit which belongs to future generations, who will inherit an exhausted, polluted planet impoverished for lack of the resources which healthy economies, and life itself, need in order to survive. All this flies in the face of the basic principles of sustainable development proclaimed at the Earth Summit in Rio de Janeiro in 1992, and confirmed at the Johannesburg Summit in 2002. After all, the fundamental principle for sustainable development is that one should live in such a way that future generations will not be left with less than we have today.

Effective conservation of natural resources within a framework of sustainable development requires:

1) More intensive effort to be put into geological surveys and recovery of natural resources; coordination of criteria for extracting deposits and a global register of these mineral resources, of forest, water and fish stocks, and of fertile soil improvements;

2) Better exploitation of natural resources, improved oil extraction and reduced losses arising from extraction and amelioration;

3) Reduction in losses arising from transportation of mineral and other natural raw materials, electrical and thermal energy, dissemination of pollution-free or low-pollution technologies, creation of autonomous joint generation installations, small generation stations, and improved oil and mining raw material processing.

For countries of the CIS it is apparent how vital these steps are. The issue is how to tackle them effectively to improve their competitiveness. An example is the offer of technology from the European Union to Kazakhstan and Russia to reduce losses derived during transportation of their mineral resources, particularly of oil and gas. But as soon as we get down to discussion of the joint arrangements required, we encounter insurmountable obstacles, since we have not yet worked out the partnership principles required, though these would work greatly to the benefit of Kazakhstan, Russia, the Eurasian Economic Union, the EU itself and the rest of the world.

A similar situation has arisen with techniques for mineral extraction. Kazakhstan and Russia inherited technologies for metallurgy and enrichment from the former USSR which we could not develop jointly because of the crisis of the 1990s; in most mining enterprises of the mining and metallurgical complex we continue to employ them to this day.

As a result, the slagheaps of the Soviet period are proliferating in the post-Soviet era, even though they incorporate not only the basic minerals but also the accompanying rare metals which are needed for the transition to the sixth stage of our technological development. The traditional extraction techniques have not given satisfactory results: they should be tied in with new cooperative partnerships which promote the transition to the requirements of the sixth technological stage of global development.

The third approach to the problem of natural resource conservation will be through alternative and renewable sources of energy and of materials. To prevent exhaustion of fuel and raw material resources, a crucial element will be their substitution on a huge scale by nuclear energy, hydrogen energy and fuel substitutes, renewable sources such as solar power and wind power, hydropower and second generation biofuels. Such substitutions must be adopted in industry, construction, transport and domestic building in all countries through joint efforts and technology transfers. This should overcome the constraints on economic growth which would be caused by the exhaustion and excessive expense of natural fuels and at the same time allow living standards to be raised.

Agreement will be needed on the criteria for an economic and ecological assessment of the various possible alternative sources of energy, taking into account the natural climatic and other features of the different countries and regions of the world. It is evident by now that the formation of such a partnership is essential, in that effort is being put into renewable energy development only in developed countries, which in itself requires enormous expenditure on research and development. Agreement on a global scale is required for the expansion of nuclear energy, since the technology has to address the twofold issue of peaceful and weapons-related nuclear technology. There is, in addition, the waste disposal factor.

ENERGY CONSERVATION

The development of world energy supplies has always been bound up with finding the most prudent and careful approach to their consumption, in which finding the best technologies for energy conservation has come to be seen as the most pressing. The demands of virtually all branches of the economy for energy in the form of oil, coal or gas have led to sharp increases in the exploitation of existing deposits, with unprecedentedly rapid exhaustion of mineral stocks. For many experts in the field, the prime task now is to discover new clean sources of renewable energy. However, there are others who believe that it will take a considerable time before new renewable sources, particularly from solar power, will be available to satisfy global demand. It may be worth recalling that the transition from one fuel source to another, in the shape of wood to coal, took some thousands of years, while that from coal to oil and gas took no more than some sixty years. From this it would follow that the next stage could be achieved in a similar timescale, allowing of course for the speed of scientific and technological progress. With this in mind, it would make sense not to exclude wood, oil and gas from our plans for energy generation over the next few decades, while seeking at the same time to introduce new sources and techniques for that purpose.

However attractive the prospects for a source such as solar power, with its simplicity and apparently unlimited abundance, we should beware of any illusions about the difficulties of introducing it on a very extensive scale. The first experimental introduction of solar power already goes back 35 years, and to date it accounts for only 1% of global consumption. The social and economic development of any country has been shown to depend on its adoption of the most economic use of energy resources, and it is for that reason that the greatest attention has been devoted in recent years in the Republic of Kazakhstan to energy consumption in the major sectors of our economy. This has included a report I have commissioned on a 'Conception for the modernization and development of housing and social welfare in the Republic of Kazakhstan.' The wake-up call for grasping the global importance of energy conservation came as a result of the crisis in the 1970s, when within ten years the price of oil increased 17 times, of gas 10 times, and of coal 3.7 times. This acted as a stimulus for national conservation programmes on a global scale, and led to a reduction in energy production by 20–40% in the space of five to ten years. Federal energy-saving programmes have been in operation in the United States since 1973. The Energy Act 2005 was adopted in

August of that year, with a timeframe of ten years or more, the aim of which was to encourage more effective use and conservation of energy resources. This included a particular concentration on the slogan 'The house with nil energy consumption'. The rationale for this was the fact that the average American home wastes 10-50% of the energy it consumes through poor insulation and ineffective use of lighting and household appliances, and hence the goal of reducing these losses by 30%.

Energy saving is a particularly pressing requirement in Japan. This is primarily because the country lacks the natural resources to satisfy its demand, particularly for oil, and must import 80% of it total requirements. A law on energy conservation took effect in 1979 which applied to the largest manufacturing enterprises, then using up 70% of the countries' energy supplies. The law imposed limits on energy use and prescribed measures to rationalise fuel consumption and to reduce heat losses in energy transmission, leading to minimum levels of unused energy resources. Any companies which failed to make the necessary efforts in this direction were subjected to heavy fines. The scope of the law was further extended in 2003. It went on to apply to other large-scale energy users such as large office buildings, department stores, hotels and hospitals. The Japanese government stipulated that by the year 2010 the amount of energy to be obtained from renewable resources should reach 1.5% of the total amount of electrical energy employed. Then the EU Summit, held in Brussels on 11–12 December 2008, adopted the 20-20-20 Plan to reduce atmospheric pollution to 20% compared to the levels in 1999 by the year 2020, to raise energy production from renewable sources to 20% of energy use as a whole, and to reduce overall losses by 20%.

In Germany, a directive on 'Energy characteristics for Buildings' took effect from the beginning of 2006, on principles reflected in the national legislation of EU countries. The original directive, as drafted by the European Parliament and the Council of the EU, stipulated that the energy effectiveness of a building is represented by the amount of energy it employs, among others, for heating, hot water, ventilation, air-conditioning and lighting. Buildings are thus to be regarded as energy systems. The provisions of the EU directive are also incorporated into national legislation relating to energy conservation. These energy-conservation measures are financed basically by German banks and major corporations, not by the state. The capital of the German Energy Agency (DENA), a limited company set up in Berlin in 2000, is a federal structure founded by the Federal Republic and a financial institution, the Credit Department for Reconstruction and Development, its rights being equally divided between the federal government and the banking group. Since 2007 the Berlin administration has been permitted to purchase vehicles for its official needs only if their petrol consumption within the city area does not exceed 6.5 litres of petrol per 100 kilometres. By 2011 the limit of permissible expense must be reduced to five years. In their acquisition of computers and other electronic equipment administrative institutions in Berlin will be obliged to select their equipment on the basis of least electrical consumption.

This is an example which we should all follow. So far as energy conservation is concerned, global estimates for the period 1986-2015 suggest that energy savings might provide two thirds of the growth of world energy requirements and by the middle of the twenty-first century it should be possible to save more fuel annually than is required to satisfy the whole of the current demand. The effectiveness of energy conservation in a country is shown by experience to be a function of the attention devoted to it by the highest levels of the national administration; on this the ranking of the country among the economically developed countries will depend, as well as the living standards of its citizens. Kazakhstan already possesses all the essential natural and intellectual resources to deal with its energy problems, and has the resource base to provide European and Asian countries with energy supplies by exporting oil, oil products and natural gas in quantities which are strategically significant for the importing countries. However, the abundance of fuel resources in our countries makes it all the more important not to be wasteful with them. Energy conservation must form part of the strategic tasks to be faced by the whole of global society, both as a means of guaranteeing energy security and as a means of maintaining high returns from the export of hydrocarbon products. The resources we need for our internal requirements should be obtainable from greater exploitation of more inaccessible deposits and by building new energy-generating plants, and with reduced expenditure by conservation at centres where the resources are actually consumed, whether in larger or smaller centres of population.

The strategic aim of energy conservation is to improve all aspects of energy use by defining the measures which may be realistically adopted to achieve it. This involves defining the measures to be taken and assessing how likely they are to be effective.

So far as energy-saving technologies are concerned, the growing cost of energy makes it essential to make their application more effective. The rapid growth of tariffs on electrical energy, gas heating and water in recent years speaks for itself. The rise in tariff levels depends above all on the growing cost of the sources of energy, the cost of the generating equipment and the transportation itself. The key requirement here is more rational use and deployment of those resources which are organic in origin, that is to say coal, oil and natural gas. Improved end use in all sectors and the development of renewable sources are vital, whether from biomass, hydroelectric power, solar power, wind power and geothermal energy or from other technologies. It is only through measures such as these, taken all together, that mankind's needs and stable development can be assured. The improvement of energy efficiency has to be seen as a matter of discovering how best to satisfy our needs for goods and services with the least possible expenditure in economic and social terms.

We must also be prepared to accept the minimal costs of

ensuring preservation of the natural environment in harmony with stable development at the local, national, regional or global level. Industrially advanced countries have the capabilities for reducing their energy use significantly without lowering their living standards or adversely affecting their economies; developing countries, by contrast, should be able to improve their overall well-being while using less energy than was the case with developed economies in time gone by. And in both groups of countries conservation will be crucial to improving both economic indicators and the quality of their overall environment. In practice it can be shown that in many instances it will be cheaper to conserve energy or avoid using it altogether than to increase its production. The implications of this are that financial resources intended to expand energy imports or extend production could actually be better directed towards other objectives, such as lifestyle improvements, better transportation systems or health-related services. Apart from the effect this might have globally on the redirection of significant financial resources, it would also benefit the productive capabilities and the competitiveness of industrial enterprises. It is noteworthy also that such development of leading-edge equipment opens the way for exports to foreign markets; it is precisely for this reason that the most advanced economies are developing intensive research programmes into energy conservation.

Kazakh researchers are also working on energy conservation, in particular on production of energy-saving lamps using super-bright light diodes, as well as carrying out industrial trials of a shortened process for the manufacture of polycrystallic silicates which can greatly reduce the cost of silicate production in solar power, while making the processes involved more ecologically acceptable. The benefits for the environment of increasing the effectiveness of such technology are evident. The energy which causes least damage to the environment may be of a kind which may not even be needed at all. In any case, when its use for particular applications can be reduced (as for example in domestic insulation, energy efficiency and the like) pollution levels will also automatically decrease in proportion.

Improved use of fuel and energy is the cheapest way to promote protection of the environment. What is more, the resulting environmental benefits are cost-free compared to the expense of introducing measures specifically for environmental protection and pollution control. Such measures should therefore be a priority in the formation of the nation's ecological policy. However, there is a clear lack of understanding and motivation when it comes to formulating energy conservation strategies and programmes to put the policies of conservation into effect. The end-user above all should know how to do this, to understand how best to achieve such results, while having some awareness of what the essential technical, financial and organisational requirements really are.

The experience of the leading industrial countries which have succeeded in raising the level of their economies through the effectiveness of their energy policy is that they need to bring to this task a whole range of special measures, in terms of administrative organization, institutions, legal structures, financial and economic mechanisms, and the scientific and technical inputs into their educational and information systems which bear on policies related to energy conservation. In each area the government concerned must have a complete grasp of the techniques required to put this knowledge into practical effect. An energy strategy which takes in a wide range of alternatives and structural reforms would not, of course, exclude exploitation of new energy sites or the construction of new power plants. That should be determined by the needs and possibilities appropriate to each specific case. A considerable proportion of energy deposits are in fact already exhausted, which will require the identification of new energy resources, if there is not to be a sharp fall in any given country's energy production. Quite some time will also be required to bring about structural reforms including new energy-saving structures. So it will be necessary to prospect for new deposits and to develop them, as well as to create new energy installations. It all depends on the scale and priorities involved. From an economic perspective it is clear that one cannot at the same time combine intensive growth in energy production and a policy of energy saving and economic reconstruction. It is already the case that a considerable proportion of all investment is going into the fuel and energy industry, and any further increase would have an extremely negative impact on other branches of the economy.

The next question relates to the form that partnerships in energy conservation should take. The options include further wholesale expansion of the energy industry, including the construction of new plant, in the expectation of some reduction in energy prices; or a policy that seeks greater economies in the energy industry. Here, experience worldwide has shown that energy-saving policies produce far better economic, ecological and social outcomes.

RENEWABLE ENERGY

Probably the best approach to overcoming the global energy crisis and establishing a thoroughly researched and ecologically sound energy policy will entail a gradual shift from a hydrocarbon-based economy to one based on renewable sources. These are generally taken to include wind energy, water-based power generation, solar power, biomass energy and power from organically derived gas, with the exception of that produced by carbon-based gasification processes. The chart on page 50 shows the share of renewable energy sources in the projected future growth of world energy production. These sources, of which solar energy forms the most important part, are expected to increase steadily and may make up more than 65% of the total by the end of the present century. The Commission of the EU plans that more than 20% of European energy sources should be derived from renewable sources by the year 2020. By 2030, with the necessary funding, this proportion could reach 50–65% on the basis of already-existing technologies. The United States plans to increase its share of power from renewable sources fivefold by 2020. Solar radiation provides a practically inexhaustible source of energy, with

1.7 x 1014 kilowatts reaching the planet's surface, which is more than 14,000 times the amount we at present consume. This colossal amount of power exceeds the limit of what mankind may actually need, which the Club of Rome calculates as 3 x 1011 kilowatts, by a factor of 500.

The whole of the solar energy which our planet receives in the course of one year reaches 1018 kilowatt hours; this is about ten times more energy than that of all established or potential sources of mineral energy, including that from fissile substances. It is worth noting that of all the solar radiation which reaches the surface of the earth, some 30% is immediately reflected back into outer space in the form of short-wave radiation, and it can be put to mankind's use with no adverse effects on the ecology of the planet. An example can be seen in the case of a heavy-energy consumer such as the city of New York, which receives twenty times more solar energy then the city needs in the course of a day. Satisfying the energy requirements of the whole planet would require a solar battery installation 600 kilometres by 600 kilometres square, which is entirely feasible from a technical point of view. The energy we currently receive from the sun's rays is 10,000 times greater than mankind will require until the year 2050. It is this kind of prospect for the generation of renewable energy which has already encouraged more than fifty countries to undertake special government programmes for that purpose. The attraction of renewable-energy supplies can be illustrated by a number of factors which include:

1) Availability in every part of the planet, and attractive as a source for all countries which can become energy independent as a result of it;

2) The fact that renewables are ecologically clean and can be used on an ever-increasing scale without negative consequences for the environment;

3) As a source of energy it is practically inexhaustible and will remain available for millions of years.

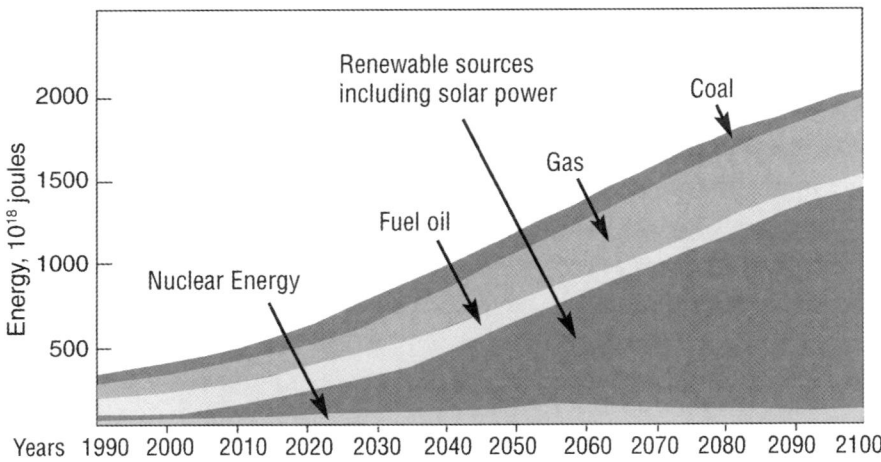

Diagram 3: **Projected development of world energy supplies**

Unlike traditional energy sources, renewables do not require large deposits to exploit, along with mining equipment, oil or gas extraction facilities and the constant purchase of transportation supplies. Their potential is also significant where there is already a large quantity of one of the inexhaustible natural sources, such as water, biomass, windy regions, intense solar radiation, geothermal sources and others. These all provide a basis for generating ecologically clean energy which does not depend on world prices for transport; as such they can promote good prospects for stable economic development, above all in developing countries where 80% of the world's population live on 30% of the world's energy supplies. The assistance these countries require can be provided by partnerships with more developed countries for the transfer of renewables technology.

Kazakhstan is second only to Madagascar in its reserves of silicates and is developing technology with the best domestic and foreign expertise to manufacture solar energy from the complete process of the silica cycle to the production of equipment with solar and thin-filmed elements.

ALTERNATIVE ENERGY SOURCES

This category of energy sources includes atomic, thermonuclear and hydrogen technologies. They differ from the traditional energy sources in that they do not involve combustion of mineral feedstock and avoid processes which cause heavy atmospheric pollution. They are 'alternative' also in the sense that in the event that the supply of mineral raw materials begins to run out, which may not be such a distant prospect, they would be well placed to replace them. Atomic energy is in a position to do this now, and thermonuclear capabilities are on the horizon. At the same time it is very important that research should continue into providing security for nuclear plants and resolving the technical problems involved with thermonuclear energy. We should first consider the prospects for atomic energy.

Most expert forecasts are for a sharp decline in the supply of hydrocarbons for energy generation within two decades or so. When that point is reached, only atomic energy will be able to satisfy the growing demand for energy for millennia still to come, without generating the greenhouse gases which are affecting the climate of the entire planet. Thus, the development of atomic energy is an inescapable prospect, if not for all countries of the world, at least for the greater number of them. The next question to be addressed is when, on what scale and in which timeframe should any given country develop its atomic energy sources. In recent times nuclear energy has come to be of great technical and economic importance. At the present time there are 442 nuclear plants in operation, with a further 30 under construction. The generating power involved amounts to around 370 gigawatts. Experience of running these installations amounts to 12,000 reactor years.

These atomic energy plants currently generate 17% of the entire world's electrical energy. Sixteen countries derive more than 25% of their energy from this source, and in France the proportion reaches around 80%.

History of global nuclear industry

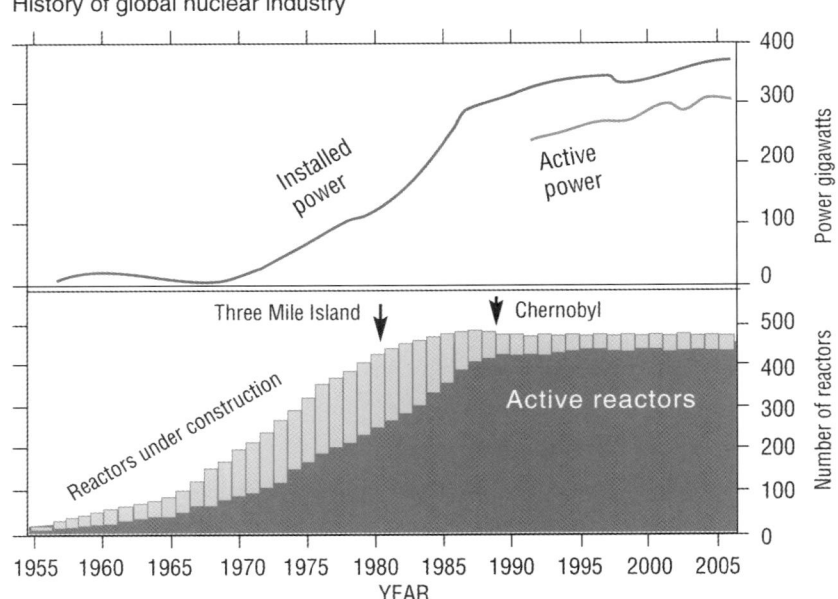

Diagram 4: **History of global nuclear energy development**
a) Summary of power from all atomic energy plants
b) Overall number of functioning atomic energy plants

The expert opinion of the International Atomic Energy Agency (IAEA) is that up to 130 new atomic power plants will be constructed by the year 2020 – though some estimates are much higher – with a combined output of 430 gigawatts, and a yearly production of up to 3020 billion kilowatt hours which could provide up to 30% of the world's energy requirements.

The world leaders in the production of nuclear energy are: the United States (788.6 billion kilowatt hours per year); France (426.8 billion); Japan (273.8 billion); Germany (158.4 billion); Russia (154.7 billion).

Diagram 4 shows that the construction of new atomic energy plants was virtually halted after the Three Mile Island accident in the United States in 1979 and the Chernobyl accident in April 1986.

This moratorium lasted until 2005 but the energy and ecological crisis which then emerged obliged many countries to review their policies towards nuclear generation and there are signs of a global 'renaissance' in that respect. The trends now observable indicate that the period of stagnation has come to an end and that new development may lead to a boom. Kazakhstan is a case in point, since we possess the necessary uranium reserves and have the specialists both for construction and management of the plants involved.

Not everything is quite so simple, however. The problem of 'dual purpose' remains to be settled, and joint efforts will be needed to ensure peaceful use of nuclear facilities. There is, however, positive experience to draw on: Kazakhstan and the international community have celebrated the twentieth anniversary of the closure of the Semipalatinsk Facility. At the same time, negative sentiment has persisted in many countries, particularly in Europe, with continuing concerns about radioactive waste and operational security. Such concerns can only be tackled through a cooperative international approach. This would have to address universally acceptable standards for waste disposal, agree on security criteria for the management of atomic energy plants which would ensure that they were safely managed and were all equipped to handle the consequences of possible future accidents. It will certainly not be possible for any one country or even group of countries to manage this process.

THE NECESSITY FOR NEW ENERGY SOURCES

Resolving the energy and ecological dilemmas we face will require the adoption of every possible means, from improving consumption patterns and efficiency in energy conservation, through innovation in the adoption of renewable and alternative energy sources to new technologies of which we can as yet have little conception. What we must do, however, is to make a start.

The need for fundamentally new energy technologies can be clearly established as follows:

1) In previous paragraphs we have examined a range of possibilities for a more rational use of natural resources and energy conservation strategies which could to some extent alleviate the energy and ecological crises. They cannot, however, provide 100% guarantees;

2) Renewable energy resources, whether from wind power, solar radiation or hydropower are much more environmentally friendly than power derived from mineral feedstocks. But the production of such energy and its delivery to the end-user demand very much greater expenditure than is the case with the traditional energy sources. At present, energy from renewables is unattractive to the business community. The significance of this is that government support for its development will be indispensable;

3) Alternative energy from atomic, thermonuclear or hydrogen power is still encumbered by unresolved problems relating to safety and waste disposal. One ton alone of processed uranium fuel creates 2,154 tons of radioactive waste products. A general conclusion is that while innovations in the development of energy-saving technologies and the development of renewable and alternative energy sources have great potential for managing the energy and ecological crises, there are as yet no obvious industrial solutions to this problem.

The countries concerned must improve their own economic competitiveness to the point where they can find industrial solutions to the energy and environmental problems which will also appeal to the business community. To take this a stage further, one could say that business is a means of manufacturing commodities which individuals find necessary and affordable. The historical record shows that almost all the problems which have faced society have been best tackled by devising technologies which transformed them by providing such essential and at the same time affordable commodities. In antiquity the problem of protecting feet from harm when walking was solved by inventing footwear, and similarly with clothing, accommodation, weapons and other such things. In our own time problems of communication have been resolved through the manufacture of mobile telephones, and cars for personal transport.

The challenges of energy and environmental protection can be met in a similar manner. Looking ahead, what we must do is to turn their management into a commodity, that is to say, with personal energy sources which are at the same time ecologically clean and are no less adapted to the requirements of the individual consumer than mobile communications equipment, cars and computers are today. Such energy devices must be designed to be convenient to use and easily accessible at all times.

Looking to such problems in a wider global perspective, we may note the efforts researchers are making to personalise energy sources. Some examples are: the 'silicon shirt' with solar batteries, increasing in the capacity of accumulators, the production of small atomic energy plants, cold thermonuclear synthesis, autonomous hydrogen-based heating systems for domestic use and so forth. However this 'personalisation' has not yet gone far enough to be of serious interest on a commercial level, a problem that can only be tackled by the global community through co-financing between governments and private partnerships.

2.3 Approaches to a global strategy for energy and the environment

In the words of N. Moiseyev: 'What is needed above all is a strategy for our civilization which is combined with the needs of the natural world. This is a qualitatively new factor in human history which goes hand in hand with the growth of human power. We are facing a crisis both of our civilization and of the world in which we live.'[3]

The necessity for such a strategy arises from the following factors:

1) First of all, the beginning of the twenty-first century has seen all the signs of a growing energy and environmental crisis on a global scale;

2) The rapid growth in energy demands cannot be satisfied in the future from mineral resources, the best of which are rapidly being exhausted;

3) Fuel costs and prices, both international and domestic, have steadily increased; this hampers economic modernization and improvements in living standards, particularly in the poorest countries and communities;

4) Attempts to tackle the fuel problem by increasing ethanol production from plant material have had the effect, in the view of many researchers, of contributing to the world food crisis;

5) The increasing level of atmospheric pollution by greenhouse gases, particularly from the expanding economies in India and China is leading to unfavourable climate changes with potentially catastrophic results;

6) Economic and geopolitical rivalries are becoming more acute, along with competition for access to energy supplies.

All these unfavourable trends are likely to persist over the next two decades, with damaging effects for stable development everywhere.

The only way out of a long period of global crisis over energy and the environment is through international partnership combining the world's best intellectual and other resources in production and consumption, of which the main features would be:

1) A large-scale transition to energy-saving technologies in production, transport, housing and social management;

2) Safeguarding unrenewable fuel resources by scrupulous management of remaining deposits, for the benefit of future generations;

3) Large-scale replacement of such deposits through the switch to alternative and renewable non-polluting sources;

4) Introduction of worldwide ecological monitoring to end the emission into the atmosphere of greenhouse gases,

with its potential for global warming and consequent climate change.

Thirdly, we must establish a range of basic innovations to secure the resource-saving technologies required by the sixth technological stage; this will require enormous investment in modernization and ecologically based production techniques, systems for the transmission and consumption of energy, and a united effort through global partnerships coordinated by the institutions of civil societies.

Achieving this is beyond the powers of any individual country or regional organisation. Only partnership on a planetary scale can achieve it. Hence there must be a greatly expanded role for the United Nations and its agencies – the UN Development Programme and UNEP – in elaborating a long-term global strategy to achieve the transition in the second half of the twenty-first century to new energy-efficient production techniques which will provide a basis for stable development.

It will then be necessary to put into effect the measures outlined in the documents approved at the G8 summit in Japan in July 2008 which were designed to overcome the energy and ecological challenges; these will need to be discussed at specialized conferences called by the United Nations, and be based on the global forecasts contained in the paper 'The future of world communities up to the year 2050' by Russian and Kazakh specialists.

THE ENERGY AND ENVIRONMENTAL STRATEGY OF THE G8
The two main international bodies concerned with the formulation of a long-term global strategy in this area are the United Nations and the Group of Eight leading industrial nations, the G8. The United Nations, together with UNEP, is currently working on ecological forecasts and strategies relating to the environment and stable development. The Stockholm Conference on the Environment, held in 1972, followed by the World Summit on Sustainable Development in Rio de Janeiro in 1992 worked on a

programme of measures to reduce pollution capable of causing environmental catastrophe on a global scale. This led to the formulation of a long-term strategy for stable development, more closely tied to the energy problem, which was consolidated and developed at the World Summit on Sustainable Development in Johannesburg in 2002. However, it was on this occasion that the International Energy Agency declared that an energy crisis was not an immediate threat to mankind: the main attention was focussed on questions relating to the implementation of the Kyoto Protocol and the situation regarding fresh water supplies to the planet. The UN's efforts were, as before, concentrated on global ecological problems as outlined in the Framework Convention on Climate Change and the Bali Action Plan.

The food crisis in 2008 obliged the UN to respond with an operational plan which was discussed at a high level conference in Rome on food security. It recommended the formation of a high-level Target Group on the global food crisis to formulate such a plan. It should be noted that the UN's activities in the field of global forecasting and strategic planning have weakened over the past decades. The department which dealt with long-term forecasting has been abolished, along with the preparatory group of experts headed by V. V. Leontyev on the prospects for world economic development up to the year 2000. UN departments are still working on long-term forecasts in the field of demographics, the environment and food supply for the period up to 2050, but not on corresponding strategic plans. The aims of the UN Millennium which focus basically on social problems do not include implementation mechanisms.

At the present time, the global centre of gravity in matters relating to strategies for dealing with the energy, environmental and food crises has increasingly shifted to the G8. The G8 summit in St Petersburg in July 2006 adopted a document on 'Global Energy Security' which laid down long-term measures designed to overcome the global energy crisis. The summit held in Germany in

June 2007 concentrated on the ecological crisis, measures to deal with climate change and on restriction of greenhouse emissions. The fullest examination of global energy, ecological and food security issues was made in documents approved at the G8 Summit in Hokkaido on 7–9 July 2008. Its main conclusions are to be found in the 'Declaration of leaders of the leading economies on questions of energy security and climate change' and 'Global Food Security'. It is there that one can find the basic elements of the current global strategy for dealing with energy, environmental and food problems in response to the challenges and crises at the beginning of the twenty-first century.

We should now turn to the basic strengths and weaknesses of this strategy:

1) The G8 representatives recognised that climate change is one of the greatest challenges mankind faces, and undertook to resist both these changes and the challenges of stable development, including security in energy supplies, food security and public health. They reaffirmed their readiness to make the necessary contribution on the basis of the UN Framework Convention on Climate Change and their commitment to the stable development strategy approved at the Rio de Janeiro conference. The latter was aimed at the three global challenges represented by the environmental, energy and food crises. From this it followed logically that the global strategy for sustainable development should be developed and refined at the Global Summit on that topic.

    I myself proposed at the General Assembly in September 2007 that a global energy and environmental strategy should be discussed at a summit meeting on stable development to be held in 2012, as a way of providing an impulse and starting point for a long-term energy and environmental strategy;

2) The timeframe for the global strategy should be fairly lengthy, let us say to the middle of the twenty-first century, as forecasts

as far as that already exist. It will, of course, be necessary to review progress over the previous ten years at successive global summits, to set new boundaries and to refine the programme;

3) We have already noted the key role of technological breakthroughs for bringing about security of energy supply, and the need for greater investment and cooperation in establishing alternative energy sources, energy conservation and more effective energy use, as well as cleaner and renewable energy sources;

4) The G8 Summit documents in 2008 devoted great attention to environmental security. They reaffirmed decisions taken at the Bali conference as a basis for reaching a global agreement in the context of the Framework Convention on Climate Change;

5) The G8 leaders welcomed the establishment of the Climate Change Fund, including the Clean Technologies Fund and the Strategic Climate Fund to be run by the World Bank, with promised contributions amounting to USD6 billion;

6) The G8 Summit document also addresses measures to halt forest degradation in developing countries, the creation of an international network to control forest exploitation and forest fires which inflict increasing damage every year to the environment, a halt to illegal logging and measures for the preservation and rational use of biodiversity;

7) Measures to be taken in relation to the environment were discussed at the Copenhagen conference on climate change in 2009;

As can be seen from the foregoing, the UN and the G8 are actively pursuing their strategy for a global policy on energy, the environment and food security, but only the first steps have been taken and they are far from responding to the scale of the growing threat. After a further study of the scenarios for development in these areas it will be necessary to formulate a scientifically researched long-term strategy for energy and the environment, and to go on from there to put it into effect, employing the principles, mechanisms and institutions of states and communities working in partnership.

THE STAGES AND MECHANISMS FOR A GLOBAL STRATEGY

The steps to be taken are illustrated in graphic form in diagram 5 (on page 62):

1) Kazakh and Russian experts have worked out a global forecast, in cooperation with researchers from other countries, of what the future holds in the field of energy supplies and the environment, together with recommendations for a global strategy to go with it. These materials were discussed at the Second Civilization Forum held in Astana on 18–19 September 2008 and when complete will be presented to the United Nations;

2) The recommendations are to be reviewed by the governments of Kazakhstan and Russia in November 2009;

3) In 2009 Russia and Kazakhstan reported to the UN on the forecast and strategic recommendations and at a conference called by the UN on energy security and climate change in 2009;

4) On the basis of a General Assembly resolution, the draft of which was presented by Russia and Kazakhstan, the Secretary General of the UN is setting up a working group composed of politicians and senior government officials, academics, representatives from the business world and environmental organisations to support the draft strategy. UNEP will perform the necessary coordination;

5) The working group will work further on the draft, discuss it at international conferences and meetings, publish it on the internet and present it for consideration at the General Assembly in 2010;

6) The General Assembly is to approve presentation of the draft by the World Summit on sustainable development 'Rio +20' in 2012. Preparation and organization for World Summit 2012 involve discussion of draft strategy and other documents on the strategic objectives of the partnership in response to the

Diagram 5: **Stages in formulation of global strategy for energy and the environment**

challenges of the twenty-first century. It would be appropriate to hold the summit in Astana, at the centre of the Eurasian landmass (previous summits having been held in Latin America and Africa). If the exacerbation of world crises were to call for an earlier date, it could be held in 2011;

7)   The documents for discussion at the summit are devoted to the energy and environmental strategies adopted by governments and intergovernmental organisations (the EU, CIS, Eurasian Economic Space, the African Union, the Shanghai Cooperation Organisation, NAFTA and others). The conclusions will be submitted to and discussed at the International Scientific Conference in 2013, celebrating the 150th Anniversary of the birth of 'noosphere' pioneer V. I. Vernadski.

A preliminary forecast of the stages of work on the strategy might be:

2013-2014   Mechanisms for strategic implementation, national and intergovernmental strategies, global programmes on individual aspects of the project;

2015-2020   Complete first stage, summing up and discussion in UN and at Global Summit, strategic adjustments;

2021-2030   Complete second stage, work on forecast and extension to period up to 2070, discussion at 'Rio +40' Summit;

2031-2040   Complete third stage, work on forecast and extension into the period up to 2080, discussion at UN and at World Summit 'Rio +50';

2041-2050   Complete next stage of strategy, work on forecast and new   version of strategy for period up to 2100, preparation and discussion at World Summit 'Rio +60';

The mechanisms for putting the strategy into effect have the following basic elements:

1)   Elaboration, refinement, extension on ten-yearly basis of long-term energy and ecological forecasts. This work to be carried out by group of international specialists coordinated by

UNESCO, through an International Scientific Council on long-term forecasting;

2) Elaboration, discussion at UN and World Summit on Stable Development of long-term energy and environmental strategy, with refinement and extension every ten years. Results of this process to be reflected in the long-term strategies of states and intergovernmental organizations;

3) Elaboration of global programmes for implementation of principal strategic objectives: energy (to be coordinated by International Energy Agency (IEA) or a specially convened organ of United Nations); environment (to be coordinated by UNEP); global projects to be assigned in accordance with overall programme.

The countries and transnational corporations which have taken part in the project programmes make up international strategic alliances which coordinate them, coordination being provided by the Economic and Social Council of the United Nations and the UN Secretary General.

Finance for the global programmes and projects is provided by the participating states and specially established global funds: the already existing Ecological Fund and the Energy and Food bodies which are being re-established under the aegis of the corresponding UN bodies. It will probably be necessary to create a special UN agency on the lines of the FAO or UNEP to provide coordination. The funds might appropriately be set up both through contributions from the participating states and from taxation of income from transnational corporations.

The most contentious problem is likely to be the imposition of obligations on governments and international bodies to reduce greenhouse gas emissions in the transition to a low carbon economy. The measures planned under the Kyoto Protocol (which expires in 2012) and by the governments of a number of countries for a trade in quotas or payments for greenhouse gas emissions, and strict rules on other emissions, have so far failed to provide appreciable results. This will necessitate new approaches which combine state and intergovernmental regulations with market incentives and taxation. Mechanisms for improved strategic partnerships will also have to be expanded, going beyond those at an intergovernmental level to transnational corporations, non-governmental environmental organisations, internet networks and other mass media, as well as involving the institutions of civil society. This strategy is very likely to require a basis in extensive innovation both for the present and for the future. This will in turn depend on understanding the new forms of technological dynamism on a worldwide scale.

CHAPTER 3

Strategy for a breakthrough in innovative technology

Human development depends on maintaining balanced and stable conditions throughout the planet, and success in achieving these can be measured by the state of the environment and mankind's well-being as a part of it.

The previous chapter of this book surveyed various aspects of a strategy for energy and the environment and the various factors which would make it possible to bring it about. Throughout the whole history of human civilization, the driving force has been the adoption of innovative technologies and the resulting transition to new, more effective ways of doing things to improve the life of human communities. In the present chapter I shall try to analyse the forces likely to affect the future course of technology, which will make possible local and global strategies capable of bringing this about.

3.1 Groundbreaking innovations and stages of technological development

To see how new technologies should be incorporated into our social and economic development it is important to have a clear understanding of what this means in practice. One of the defining factors – new technologies or technological innovation – emerges from scientific and technological activities whose incorporation into various branches of production and management proves to be economically effective – and/or significant – from a social or ecological point of view. Many other definitions are possible, but a feature shared by all new types of technology is their ability to improve labour productivity, to increase incomes and to reduce levels of poverty.

In the first half of the twenty-first century we stand on the threshold of a technological revolution. A distinguishing feature of this period is likely to be the emergence of groundbreaking innovations from new forms of production in post-industrial technologies. For a worthy response to the challenges of post-industrial technology the techniques of production must possess a number of new characteristics. In the first place the technology must acquire a more human dimension. Such a process might proceed in three directions:

1) Automatic processes, robots and information technology all help to free workers from heavy physical and boringly repetitive tasks, so that they can concentrate on their use of intellectual processes, planning and the creative capacities of the machines and technologies they are employing. This presupposes a range of basic innovations which alter the nature of production and the human contribution to it;

2) An increased role for innovations facilitates expanded production of high-quality goods and services for individual consumers, thereby directly satisfying the constantly increasing material and spiritual demands of the population;

3) A relative, and at a later stage complete, reduction of weapons production, along with the innovations they require, which have had such prominence in our industrialized society.

In the second place, as has been demonstrated by Kazakh and Russian scientists in their forecasts for energy and environmental developments in the period up to 2050, the distinguishing feature of post-industrial technology and innovation will be the concentration, through environmental policies, on a more rational interaction between natural forces and human society. Human invention and its expression in technological innovations have begun to affect the biosphere to such an extent that natural processes are no longer self-sustaining. They may not even function without human ecological inputs, while the way we have interfered with the environment has already led in some cases to ecological disaster. If we are to restore some balance to the interaction between natural and social activities so that humanity can actually survive, three new technological approaches will acquire particular importance:

1) Ensuring that natural resources are used in production in the most sophisticated possible ways, and that waste management methods are more widely employed in their extraction, processing, transport and consumption;

2) Reducing environmental pollution, and cutting harmful emissions into the atmosphere and water supplies;

3) Adoption of renewable forms of energy and natural raw materials, regeneration of raw material resources, through geological prospecting, forest and water management, soil improvement and reclamation, and so on.

In the third place, technological innovations should be made available on a global scale by disseminating them beyond national boundaries. A global market in technologically advanced goods and services should accelerate the adoption internationally of the most important innovations, bring together the resources of the international community and extend the scale of the income to be derived from high technology.

In the fourth place, efforts should be made to abbreviate the life cycle of technological innovation, by speeding up innovation in production methods through the introduction of new machinery and technical processes. Expert opinion expects the duration of Kondratyev cycles, together with the technology they require, to contract from 50–60 to 40–45 years in the post-industrial age. Generations of technology succeed one another, introducing scientific discoveries or big technical advances (or individual developments which together open a path to such advances) in the main fields perhaps once in a decade; they are tied to scientific developments and discoveries which emerge, with some delay, over a similar period. New generations of technology do not take shape straight away in a complete or widely accessible form. They are preceded by long periods of incubation, with scientific investigation of some promising technological concept. This then needs patents, preparation of experimental models or industrial sets of equipment, machine-building and subsequently marketing research and placement.

It is only after this that the key innovations can become established. At first they secure only a fairly narrow range of advanced applications, but then are quickly disseminated as a result of what seems like a landslide of improvements; these in turn adapt the new technological breakthroughs to meet the demands of the market, leading to increases in scale and resultant profits.

In the fifth place, production methods in the post-industrial age must seek to align the time scales and levels of innovative technology within the various branches of industry and countries across the planet. The degree of inequality which at present exists will require that innovations are made universally available.

The nature and impact of new waves of innovation result in a shift to a new level of technology, with a structure which is itself internally complex. This can be summarised as follows:

1) An independent sequence of production processes is combined with interconnecting processes concerned with delivery and consumption; this makes up an aggregate of technologically linked production – a technological aggregate – the linking of whose elements represents their technical homogeneity;

2) Connected by productive cooperation, technologically adapted to one another and possessing a relatively homogeneous level of technology, they represent a complex of interlinked technological aggregates – a technological structure;

3) Basic technological aggregates form the core of a technological structure;

4) Technological innovations which contribute to the formation of the core of a technological structure have been given the name of a 'key factor' in the branches which drive the process. The growth of these branches depends on the spread of the technological innovations in the leading branches of industry to which those branches refer. These make intensive use of the 'key factor' and are best adapted to its use. For each structure it is possible to define a period of domination, technological leaders, the core of a technological structure, its advantages in comparison with its predecessor, the fundamental institutions and the organization of innovatory activity in the leading countries. A typical phenomenon in the economy of any country is a multi-structural nature, that is to say that there exist simultaneously in the various sectors of an economy various structures which act upon one another;

5) The predominant one, which defines the level reached in competitiveness and the effectiveness of its production and technology;

6) The structure which replaces it, which is to be found in the phase in which its innovations are being adopted;

7) A displaced structure which, however, retains its strength in some sectors of the economy;

8) Old structures still surviving.

A current expert assessment is that the dominant force is that of the fifth technological stage under the leadership of the United States, Japan, Germany, Sweden, the European Union, South Korea, Canada and Australia. At its core are electronics, computing and optoelectronics, software, telecommunications, robot construction, gas production and processing and information services.

The expectation is that the core of the sixth technological stage will most probably be renewable energy, nanotechnology and photonics, gene engineering and biotechnology, as applied to animals and subsequently to humans. Substantial new information systems will be developed on a global basis, extending to the sciences, the environment, education, social and cultural applications and others. The emergence of new stages is generally accompanied by changes in the make-up of the technological leaders as well, which is also likely in the first half of the present century. In forecasting the likely structure and epicentre of the sixth stage, the specialists assume that it will fully reflect the basic technological features of post-industrial production methods, including the human, spiritual and intellectual underpinnings which accompany them.

3.2   New technologies: their trends and perspectives

Technological innovation has tended to develop in recent decades against a background of:

1)   An increasing gap between leading countries and societies and more backward ones;

2)   Sharper competition in global markets;

3)   New challenges from population pressures and from problems with energy supply and the environment;

4)   Stresses within globalisation as a result of innovative technologies.

These trends are conditioned by the introduction of new techniques and technological modifications displacing older ones, though with less and less profit accruing from the innovations themselves. The first trend in global technological development became apparent because the shift to the sixth technological stage and its post-industrial production methods have required a radical renewal of the world's productive capital resources, with the necessary investments being made in basic innovation. But this is at a time when the pace of effective global regeneration is slowing down, because as the technological machine becomes more powerful and extensive the forces of inertia within the system actually increase. This technological stage, therefore, seeks to reproduce itself, with modifications, within more extensive parameters. As technologies outlive their historical span and become obsolete, the number of innovations needed to improve them also increases. Delay in making such improvements obstructs the introduction of the new technological stages, just when investments are needed to bring in new technologies on the necessary scales and within the right timeframes. The critical situation which has arisen in global technological development is paralleled by the drop in the rate of productivity. The way to resolve this situation will be to raise the volume of investment in scientific and technological renewal and its share of GDP, so as to redistribute resources for the innovation programmes of the next sixth stage of global technological development.

Current levels and growth in investment for environmental and humanitarian purposes are a quite inadequate response to the enormous human and conceptual challenges they pose for our society in the post-industrial period, most particularly for low-income countries. The second trend in our overall technological development is the concentration we observe on industrial priorities such as military development and ever greater exploitation of nature's resources. This does nothing to satisfy the broader needs of society and more backward countries in the post-industrial age. Our technologically orientated economy has grown many times in the course of its current phase, with its concentration of investment on innovation in industry and the exploitation of natural resources. This trend has been reinforced by greater capitalization and its influence on the build-up on a global scale of transnational companies located, for the most part, in developed countries. Changing this emphasis would have to come about by restructuring strategies for investment and innovation, by raising its share of GNP and concentrating more on human capital and technologies for resource conservation.

The third trend is marked by the steadily increasing gap between advanced and less advanced countries and communities. This can be seen in the latter's low competitiveness, and the gulf between

	Advanced technology exports		R&D expenditure as percentage of GDP	Information and communication expenditure	
	Millions of US dollars	% of global total		% of GDP	dollars per head
Global total	1,243,114	100	2.28	6.8	538
Low income countries			0.73	5.9	41
Middle income countries	332,483	26.7	0.85	5.4	149
High income countries	910,631	73.3	2.45	7.2	2,466

Diagram 6: **World Bank advanced technology exports**[5]

affluence and destitution in different parts of the world. The most recent stage in technological development, the sixth, as compared to the previous one, has deepened the contrast between developed and the least developed countries, which lack even the minimum scientific, investment and human resources to move on to the next stage. The gravity of the situation is borne out by World Bank statistics on the export of high technology, the expenses involved in creating it, and the costs of scientific research and development, including information and communications technology.

The only way out of this situation lies in a partnership between developed and poorer communities, by ensuring that the latter can be given the means to bridge the gap which divides their levels of economic and social development.

The fourth trend, technologically speaking, is to be found in the shortage of qualified personnel at the fifth level of technological development: that is to say the lack of scientists, construction workers, engineers, technicians and qualified workers, managers, and government officials who can put the new technologies into practical effect. The phase of partial improvements to industrial technologies is coming to an end. Worsening conditions and the challenges of the twenty-first century make it essential to adopt a wide range of basic innovations, well funded with starting capital, for the sixth, post-industrial, stage of development. The necessary breakthrough will not occur without committed innovators and the partnership of state institutions, big business, and leading scientists and educators. To establish such partnerships in all parts of global society will be a major task for decades to come, without which it will not be possible to achieve technological transformation on a scale more evenly distributed worldwide than the industrial revolution which preceded it. This is one of the core elements in the partnerships needed in coming decades, since the new technological stage must have a whole range of innovatory breakthroughs as its foundation.

This global technological revolution must have a scientific basis capable of rapidly taking on the large-scale technologies of the sixth stage, primarily in branches of the economy receptive to innovation, such as vital sectors like food supply, energy, information technologies, and in education, culture and public health.

In order to give effect to these long-term forecasts and the strategies for which they provide the basis, a prerequisite will be scientific discoveries and major inventions which will open the door to critical new technologies and possibilities for social development. This is most likely to come about in developed countries, but in that case it will be essential for the progress they achieve to be made available throughout the world. The three societies already benefitting from high incomes which are best equipped to do this from the necessary scientific and technical points of view are: North America (the US, with 4,605 researchers per million inhabitants,

21.2% of patent applications and 7.1% of income from sale of patents); Western Europe (corresponding figures 2,607, 8.4% and 7.6%) and Japan (5,287, 41.4% and 14.3%)). Apart from Japan, North Korea and China, Asian countries lack significant scientific and technical potential and depend for the most part on borrowing from others. Russia's scientific potential is substantial, with 3,319 researchers per million inhabitants, but in practical terms it is well behind with 2.6% of patent applications and 0.21% in terms of royalties and licensing. Nonetheless, the superiority of the most developed countries has its downside, in that the bulk of its research is directed to improvements in the innovations characteristic of the fifth technological stage. The majority of countries are not in a position to rely on their own scientific and technical resources to achieve technological breakthrough, and are obliged to import it. The partnerships we have been discussing must therefore be based on massive technology transfers from the advanced countries to those which are less so, on a basis of mutual advantage to which both sides are committed. Moreover, the less advanced must develop their own capacities for absorbing and adapting the necessary breakthroughs, by themselves acquiring the necessary scientific and technological skills.

The various communities on the Eurasian landmass have a particular role to play so far as advanced technologies are concerned. They possess a sufficiently well-developed scientific base and educated workforces to be able, not just to borrow technology, but also to adopt a leadership role in a number of directions. They must also, however, be consistent in their pursuit of innovation, with considerably expanded investment both by the state and by private business if they are to achieve the necessary breakthroughs. Thus, a country like Kazakhstan should seek to concentrate its efforts on no more than a certain number of high priorities. A new wave of innovation will also require revamped investment structures, substantial commitment to research, adoption and dissemination of advanced technologies of the sixth stage, and reallocation of investment in advanced and fast-developing branches of technology. At an early stage, such investments carry a high risk and then a long period of recoupment; it follows that they require more substantial input from government during the start-up period. This relates not just to domestic investment but also to direct foreign investment which is needed for high technology transfer. Priority here must be given to technologies which make national innovation systems easier to introduce.

It is apparent from this that global development requires adoption of innovative mechanisms to promote partnership, designed to speed up and universalize sixth stage technologies directed at critical areas in food supply, energy provision, the environment, fighting serious diseases and epidemics, and in the field of education. Such an approach needs long- and medium-term forecasts of innovation strategies by region and by individual country. International organisations have made long-term projections for population trends, food supply, and the environment for the period up to the year 2050. The Rand Corporation has made its own forecasts for the global technological revolution up to 2020. The Institute for Economic Strategies and the Pitirim Sorokin-Nikolai Kondratyev International Institute have drawn up and published a projection of innovation in Russia for the period up to 2050, with particular reference to energy and the environment, and to social and cultural factors. Such projections must be periodically updated and amended to take account of new challenges and openings. The separate elements of the scientific and technological forecasts for the planet as a whole are thus due to be fulfilled in Kazakhstan on the basis of international trends.

We need to take into account technology forecasts for the planet as a whole and develop partnerships in developing long-term global strategies for technological renewal in the most urgent directions (in energy and the environment, nano- and biotechnologies, new materials, transport, information technology and so on). These can be worked out with reference to the long-term forecasts and discussed at the UN General Assembly and the Global Summit on Stable Development.

Another requirement is to forge a partnership between leading and less developed countries in the development of science and technology on a global basis, including the way this affects human development. Successive changes in scientific development and the application of new technologies, particularly as society becomes more knowledge-based, will also demand diversification of infrastructures and generational changes, including in the structure and level of the qualifications required of researchers, construction workers, engineers, technicians, managers and workers. This is a particularly acute problem for backward communities with high levels of illiteracy and a very limited pool of graduates. Given the high demands needed to progress to the sixth technological stage it is obvious that the least developed countries and communities are in no position to achieve the necessary breakthroughs on their own: they need assistance on a huge scale from the most advanced.

The basic requirements here were formulated in the document approved in St Petersburg at the G8 Summit on 16 June 2006 on 'Education for innovatory societies in the twenty-first century.' The document states that 'An innovatory society prepares its citizens for life in conditions of rapid change. We shall encourage the formation of an innovatory society by means of development and integration of all three elements of the "Triangle of Knowledge" (education, research and innovation), large-scale investment in human resources, the development of professional practices and scientific research, as well as methods supporting modernisation in the systems of education so as to correspond more closely to the needs of a global, knowledge-based economy. As science is globalized, along with technology and the economy, international cooperation in the training of highly qualified personnel and the accumulation of knowledge becomes essential to meet global challenges.'[6]

3.3 Scientific basis of a global strategy for innovation and technological breakthrough

ROLE OF FORECASTING IN INNOVATION AND TECHNOLOGY

Forecasting likely developments in companies, countries and whole communities has recently come to be better understood, appreciated and followed through. Literally all countries are trying to refine their views of the future, while global and regional organizations are seeking to build up pictures of their overall prospects to the year 2050 and beyond. The data behind such prognoses must, however, be open to question, as must the extent to which they can put into effect.

There is now a universal awareness of the deep crisis which the world is facing, most markedly over the past three years in relation to the financial system, the environment, energy resources and food supplies, these being the factors which bear most directly on human development. These negative developments have been experienced by the bulk of the world's population, but all the strength of intergovernmental organisations and the resources of the world's leading countries have proved insufficient to fend them off, and even now coordinating the necessary action to deal with them seems impossible. One has the clear sensation that the forecasts made by individual states and intergovernmental organizations, based as they are on national and global interests, diverge to a significant extent from the objectives and actions of the transnational companies. But it is the latter on which much of the financial stability, environmental security, development in science and technology, indeed human development as a whole, has come to depend.

We all need to look carefully at the role of governments in bringing about breakthroughs in innovation and technology, and then find ways to improve the means by which states and international organisations give effect to the forecasts and strategies they have drawn up. We have to ask what the basic features are of such forecasts of technological development across the globe, bearing in mind that it is such developments which provide the material conditions for social and economic progress overall. Countries which formerly did not have the capacity to take part in the processes of innovation and adoption of new technologies, or to absorb the benefits of scientific and technological progress achieved elsewhere are now suffering from insufficient human potential. Thus, they become a source of serious concern to more technically and socially advanced members of the international community through the problems they create with migration, spread of disease, terrorism or religious extremism. How should the most advanced states concentrate their long-term strategies for scientific and technological development?

It must be admitted that there has been little change in the view of the technological future worked out in the course of the past decade: it has, of course, become more detailed, with a clearer understanding of possible new applications of fundamental discoveries made in the latter years of the twentieth century. There is an expert consensus that the basic features of the sixth technological stage, succeeding that now reached by the world's leading countries, will embrace nanotechnology and nanomaterials, biotechnology, information technology and artificial intelligence, cosmic technology and renewable energy. The scientific basis for development in these areas will come from fundamental and applied research on renewable energy sources, transformation of materials into new substances and cell modification in living organisms, including gene engineering. However, we have to take note of the fact that for all the promise held out by such industrial approaches and the scientific research involved, developing them on a global scale is hedged about with a large number of 'buts'.

I have already referred to the fact that the transition to the new technological stage depends on fundamental discoveries made in the course of recent decades. It is generally accepted practice in the scientific community that fundamental research belongs to the whole world: it is not the property of any one individual and, as a consequence, scientists, companies or states are not limited in their application of such knowledge to developing their national economy. But it is precisely in this area that problems are beginning to emerge over the application in various countries of particular fields of fundamental knowledge. The countries of North America, Western Europe and Japan are unquestionably the leaders in transforming fundamental research into practical applications for the manufacture of finished products or processes. Whether for subjective or objective reasons or because of external or internal factors, other countries lack the ability to achieve such transformations and are, therefore, obliged to employ products or applications made by companies in the advanced countries. This disproportion is beginning to make itself felt in scientific and technological development and consequently in inequalities in human development.

The fact is that in the leading countries of the world it is government corporations and private companies, with their concentration on raising their efficiency levels, which are the driving force behind the adoption of advanced applications of scientific and technological processes to achieve overall economic progress. But the nature of these processes is different according to whether a country is already developed or is in the process of development. Production, employment of high technology goods and services, and work directly connected with the creation of new technologies are concentrated primarily in the developed countries. Whereas in developing countries, the consumption of such goods and services depends on the ability of the economy to use and to pay for them. On top of that, it is in the developing countries that the least clean advanced technology processes are used. The consequent divide in the use of innovatory and high technology products brings about disproportions on a global scale in human, environmental and economic development, which have exacerbated the grave crises we are now facing. Developed countries are suffering the effects of financial 'bubbles' (or virtual capital), ecological over-consumption and energy dependence.

Developing countries, on the other hand, are suffering from the ecological effects of production, from weakening demand for raw materials and inadequacies in health care, cultural provision and education. Developing countries simply cannot adapt for the benefit of their economies the innovations and benefits of scientific research to which the transnational companies and private businesses in developed countries have access.

It is worth remembering that when discussions take place on the transition to the sixth technological stage, most countries involved are still making use of production methods from the first technological stage while trying to introduce practices appropriate to the fifth stage. While one part of the world's population is making the transition from the consumer society to one marked by innovation and intellectual activities, the greatest demand being for quality of life, the remaining part is compelled to seek help with food supplies and coping with diseases on an enormous scale.

One of the weightiest causes of the contradictions we see in global society is that the responsibility for pursuing fundamental research is taken over by nation states, while the management of applied technology is taken over by the private companies of the most prosperous ones. As a result, cutting edge scientists are not working on the technological problems of developing countries, including those relating to the environment, manufacturing and social questions, since they are of no interest to commercial companies. It seems to me that it is precisely this aspect of global development which should be tackled by an active partnership between governments. It should be regarded an essential factor in stable development and should exclude the possibility of further contradictions arising over technology and in human development in the various regions in the world. It should be noted that in resolving issues connected with technological development the developing countries are on their own. Furthermore, they are obliged to remain more closely linked to the transnational corporations, which are concerned with raw material deliveries and the sale of goods for everyday use, which amounts to preserving a dependent relationship between colonies and the metropolitan power.

The governments of developed countries for their part are more concerned with the effective operation of global transnational corporations which raise the quality of consumption for their own populations. The example provided by South Korea, Singapore and China which have made the leap from backwardness to high levels of innovation and technological development is one which should be followed by all developing countries. At present there is no intergovernmental body with the powers and responsibility which would enable it to regulate technological development on a global scale. Of course, it is the case that organisations like UNDP, UNIDO (the United Nations Industrial Development Organisation), regional bodies in Europe, Africa and the Pacific region are both active and have achieved some success within their own areas. But their capacities do not extend beyond the limits of interaction, consultation, programme formulation, the organization of conferences, seminars and the like.

In this connection it would probably be appropriate to consider in the first instance some changes in the powers and available mechanisms available to the United Nations to promote technological development on a global level. The results of investigations into the scientific and technological problems of developing countries should then be reformulated as specific tasks for the global community to address. It should also be so arranged that participation in such undertakings should be for experts from developed as well as developing countries. This would do a great deal to combine two separate processes which do not normally combine because of disparities in their respective levels of operation: that is to say the direction normally taken by scientific research at the advanced level and inadequate scientific expertise in developing countries. A point of particular importance is that of inventors' rights to the results of their own research, which might be taken over by the UN to benefit developing countries and regions. While acknowledging and safeguarding the scientists' and co-workers' direct ownership of the processes involved, it should be established that access to technologies which are of vital importance to resolving the social and economic problems of developing countries should be available without charge. If the UN were able to do this, it would help to direct intellectual potential towards making technological development more fairly distributed and to correcting imbalances, while opening the way for improved conditions in the future.

BASIS FOR STRATEGIES FOR TECHNOLOGICAL BREAKTHROUGH

Without going into too much detail about the competitiveness of national economies it should be stressed that a large number of countries in the world dispose of productive elements from all five stages of technological development, which are developed and effective to varying degrees. If we assume that the technological development of a country basically defines its level of social and economic development, all countries should make efforts to join in the process which leads to the threshold of the sixth stage of technological development. The economy of each individual country is different from all the others, and the most important task for governments and societies is to establish the right entry point into the next technological stage and identify the factors which are likely to make the process best suited to their individual development.

The next technological stage, the sixth, has some particular features, the most fundamental being the many different branches of its scientific programmes, as in nanotechnology, biosciences and information technology, which extend into literally every part of the economy. Thus, depending on its technological advantages each country must be ready to be, not an observer on the sidelines, but an active producer of goods which draw on the very latest technological means. At present, the scientific and industrial community in Kazakhstan is moving in that direction. With an economy clearly oriented towards raw material production we are at present carrying out a series of programmes to develop five particular priorities in science and industry. They include nanotechnology and new materials, biotechnology, informatics and space technology, the hydrocarbon and ore-mining sector and its associated services, as well as atomic and renewable energy. While we do not seek to diminish the importance of other industrial sectors, we have concentrated our attention on the scientific and technological sectors in which the Kazakh economy is particularly strong and which coincide with key areas of development at the sixth technological level. In order to achieve the results we want in the sciences, we are carrying out a series of reforms which can raise the effectiveness of each of the factors which will ensure that Kazakhstan can reach this level:

1) By increasing substantially the level of funding for scientific research and innovatory projects;

2) Taking steps to stimulate co-financing from the private sector for scientific and technology projects;

3) Setting up five major national scientific laboratories based on the existing leading institutes and fifteen engineering laboratories at the universities with five specific scientific priorities;

4) By attracting foreign scholars of global standing in the establishment of scientific priorities;

5) By changing the science management system, so that scientific organizations become shareholders closely allied to the commercial sector;

6) By creating management holdings in the scientific sector to allow scientific organizations to exercise greater influence on the economy, primarily through scientific projects organised jointly with private companies;

7) By organising a Science Fund set up as a joint-stock company specifically for co-financing scientific projects designed to improve production and create new goods with new characteristics;

8) By creating and applying measures to protect scientists' intellectual property rights which will rule out plagiarism and malicious borrowing of scientific ideas;

9) By changing the system for setting up projects in applied science, now to be directed at addressing current and projected technological problems in Kazakh enterprises.

Such conditions for scientific activity in Kazakhstan create the basis for changing the direction of scientific knowledge. In earlier times the basic tendency was for Kazakh scientists to take part in foreign and international projects; each year now an increasing number of foreign scholars are contributing to such work in Kazakhstan itself.

The established scientific priorities need to be refined with regard to the specific fields covered, and manufacturing and project creation. We are now carrying out a large study in the framework of the globally well-established 'Foresight' methodology which makes it possible to formulate development aims not only for science, but also for industry, and for basic branches of the economy, the state, for investors and in the field of education.

3.4 Global experience in applying new technologies

SCIENTIFIC AND TECHNOLOGICAL ACHIEVEMENT OF BREAKTHROUGHS IN INNOVATION

The scientific level reached by each country is one of the fundamental influences on its social and economic development; it also defines the position it occupies in the world's economic system. Studies have shown that these levels and the technical innovations connected with them have laid the foundations for the prosperity and well-being of societies across the globe. For this reason, studying the scientific and technical systems adopted by individual countries and the extent of their development has become an important scientific discipline in its own right.

The level of scientific and technical development reached in each case plays a large role in the economic and social/political development of separate countries as well as of the world community as a whole. The level and quality of individuals' lives are traditionally conditioned by the extent of the economic development reached in a given country and its social structures which go with it. The higher the level of development in the social and economic life of the country and the higher the level of security it provides to defend the individual from unfavourable circumstances and other dangers, the better the average longevity in the country as a whole.

The development of advanced technologies in particular sectors of each industry and the way these are employed by it determines the overall state of the world market, and the ranking of individual countries within it. Overall, the volume of production within the science-intensive sectors of the world market amounts in value to around USD2.5 to 3 trillion, in excess of the value of the raw materials and energy markets. There has been a consistent trend towards ever-increasing growth in processing sectors with a high scientific content. In countries like the US and Japan the growth in national income has reached 65–80% thanks to the output of the science and technology sector. The total value of technology output is now reckoned to be about 60% of all GDP and its rate of growth exceeds that of sales of other products.

Thus in the 1990s the total global trade in technology was calculated to amount to a figure in the range of USD20–50 billion, while in the year 2000 the total already stood at around USD500 billion. Trade in technology products is characteristically very profitable, with production costs amounting to only 10–25% of the total of goods sold. Once a firm possesses the necessary technology it can reach world levels of quality production in a relatively short period of time and highly competitive returns; it can then acquire new markets and thus increase its export levels. It is calculated that for each US dollar expended on the import of a foreign technology licence the return in the US is around USD6.2, the UK 3.1, France 5.4, Japan 16, which can then be invested in research and development. In addition to this, the purchaser acquires the capacity to carry out independent research separate from the levels of scientific and technological content he/she has bought, and to overcome any backwardness in other sectors. The development of new technologies and goods from what is usually systematic investment in research and development is carried out overwhelmingly in high-income OECD countries and in a limited number of Asian and Latin American countries.

OECD countries, which make up 14% of the world's population, have had registered 86% of all patent applications worldwide. These countries provide more funds for research and development in both absolute and relative terms: on average 2.4% of GNP compared with Kazakhstan's 0.26%. For the US the figure is 2.84%, Sweden 3.8%, Korea 2.8%, Finland 3.5%, Japan 3.04% and Germany 2.44%. It should also be noted that considerable resources have been put into research and development by the private sector. To take one example, during the Soviet period the system employed in Kazakhstan to manage scientific and technical activity was through the state, for both science and industry, and it worked very effectively. What is the situation now? With the transfer of the country's industry to the private sector, amounting now to 90%, the link between science and production has been lost, and industry has ceased to concern itself with scientific research. In this situation the state authorities have understood the need for scientific and technological development, and devote financial means to scientific development, but the results of the scientific work have basically been overlooked and are not made use of in production, not because they are bad, but because the private industrial sector is not interested. And industry, for its part, is not interested in them either, not because they do not need scientific innovations but because the results of the research are not brought to the point where they can be put to use. The resulting situation is that the private side of the economy works on its own and buys the technology it needs from abroad ready for use, with the result that it becomes dependent on foreign technologies. There is also a clear misalignment between the financing of innovations by the state, with 90%, and the private sector, with only 10%.

For Kazakhstan it has been an important aim to bridge the gulf between the sciences and the processes of production. For this purpose our experts have worked out how to release our potential in science and technology by means of state and private sector partnerships between scientific organizations and Kazakh industrial enterprises. As part of this process government bodies work with the private sector to identify the priorities and work with authorised agencies to establish government-backed projects through scientific and technical programmes organized at the national level. Depending on how the programmes work out the most promising ones are selected for adoption with co-financing between the Science Fund and the private sector. Thus the private sector participates through its partnership with the state in setting up the scientific projects it needs, provides co-financing and then makes use of the results. Experience from elsewhere in the world indicates that depending on how they are selected and put into effect, it is possible to identify innovative approaches through which the countries concerned introduce and disseminate knowledge – what one might call innovating countries.

Another element is what might be called imitative development, designed to enable the country concerned to 'catch up', of which a striking proponent was originally Japan, followed by a whole host of Asian 'dragons' who came to be known as 'copycat' countries. This approach involves precise identification of economic tasks from which a selection can be made of advanced technologies which can then be developed and put into production. One of the basic preconditions for this to work effectively is the availability of a large, low-paid and mostly well-qualified workforce. This approach does, however, have its limitations, as can be seen from what happened with Japan in the 1990s. When its rate of economic growth sharply dropped it began to change over exclusively to a programme of innovation and shifted its emphasis to creating new fields of knowledge.

In choosing their areas of specialization it should be noted that states with advanced levels of technology do not usually sell to others 'breakthrough' technologies of strategic importance which may prove to be important for their future development. So any state which aims to embark on innovative policies must in one way or another create an effective knowledge-based sector which does not necessarily have to be particularly large. One of the basic criteria when selecting priority areas for scientific research has to be environmental security. When defining the priority the following factors also have to be taken into account:

1) The degree to which it affects the environment, human health and any other long-term implications;

2) The impact of up-to-date technologies for conservation of resources, which can guarantee a closed cycle of economic activity, economize on natural resources and preserve the local environment.

The adoption of new technologies on this basis will improve the health of the environment, and have beneficial effects on public health; advances in biotechnology can also make possible new medicines for the treatment of a variety of illnesses.

With the current globalization of economic life, developed countries can secure their development by further improvement of existing technologies, technical methods and the introduction of new scientific inputs which will provide their citizens with a decent standard of living. And, as their economies grow in stable conditions and with rising incomes, the country can also enjoy the benefits of technological progress.

Resolving this problem successfully will also carry with it increased benefits from scientific development and new technologies. In particular, it will make possible not only economic advantages, but will also facilitate up-to-date, highly effective and competitive technologies which can satisfy the needs of the average consumer. Such developments must also meet the requirements of the population, help to deal with ecological problems and facilitate progress in medicine, pharmaceuticals, machine building and instrument production (for both ecological and scientific use), food industry and agriculture, informatics and building.

The development of new technologies should result in stable economic conditions and breakthroughs deriving from the insights and achievements of the sixth technological stage, and also from partnership between countries in transferring advanced technologies, and from improvements in the quality of living, based on resolution of the following issues:

1) Construction of more well-equipped working environments for scientists and production and service personnel;

2) Improvement in education levels, increasing the proportion of the population engaged in more highly qualified work which will reward them with higher incomes;

3) Use of the latest technology to resolve outstanding production, environmental and social problems;

4) Expansion of research to benefit production of consumer goods, medicines and other products, in order to increase supplies for our domestic markets of high quality, competitively priced and easily available items;

5) Increase in budget allocations at various levels to expand production levels of research-intensive goods and raise income for the average citizen;

6) Increase the provision of new equipment which will provide improved amenities in the workplace, improve working conditions and reduce damage to individuals and the environment as a whole.

RISK PREVENTION IN INTRODUCTION OF NEW TECHNOLOGY

While the new technology can have beneficial effects for society it can also generate risks which have to be taken into account. During the period of particularly intensive industrialization in the first half of the twentieth century, the associated breakthroughs in some forms of technology led to increased risks in general, including new kinds of problems which were due to the nature of the new technology itself. At an early stage in this industrial development it was connected with new working practices and methods which directly affected the workers involved. After the emergence of technologies which were particularly complex, as, for example, at nuclear power stations and at some weapons-manufacturing and chemical plants, the dangers came to extend beyond the premises in which these various operations were being performed. Risks of this kind have now come to be a constant factor hanging over individuals, society as a whole and the global environment itself. In other words, they have become a social and environmental threat which extends to the whole planet. As technologies developed on a massive scale in the nineteenth and twentieth centuries, the values which evolved with them came to embrace the view that new inventions represented the highest point creativity in science and technology could reach. At the same time, the value of any particular invention was associated with the income it could generate or the destruction it could cause, depending on its application to civilian life or its value in warfare.

The consequence of this was that by the beginning of the twenty-first century a number of inventions had been employed in such a way as to inflict harm on the whole of mankind. The only way out of the social and economic crises we now face will be a fundamental reassessment of our value system, which must include a fresh look at the way we interpret creativity in the sciences and technology. The main consideration must now be not just the discovery or invention in its own right but the analysis we make of all the consequences which may flow from putting it to use, whether environmental, medical, civic and social, cultural, ethical or economic, with the broadest perspectives kept clearly in view.[7] Having spent all its historical development on warfare or preparations for it, mankind has now, however, changed its views enough to embark on the road to arms limitation, to the point of renouncing the most dangerous forms of military technology.

An example is the decision taken by Kazakhstan to renounce the possession of nuclear weapons in order to provide security to its own population and to strengthen peace in the world. After the collapse of the Soviet Union a considerable stock of nuclear weaponry remained in Kazakhstan: strategic rockets with multiple warheads, which in the West were given the menacing name 'Satan', long-range bombers and the atomic and thermonuclear weapons which went with them. At the time the whole of this deadly arsenal ranked fourth in firepower in the whole world, and Kazakhstan had on its territory 148 underground installations for the launch of surface-to-surface intercontinental ballistic missiles. These launching-pads contained 104 intercontinental ballistic rockets each of which carried a nuclear warhead. Each rocket weighed 7.6 tons and its strike radius was around twelve thousand kilometres. Kazakhstan also possessed a considerable stock of biological weapons. For the first time in history, Kazakhstan took the voluntary decision to renounce the whole of this devastating arsenal, a worthy contribution by independent Kazakhstan to global stability and security. Consequently, it should be possible in a similar fashion to deal with industrial and agricultural technologies which could also have an undesirable impact on the earth's environment.

The scientific knowledge we now have is of a high level, with an accessible base of information in all branches of knowledge, and industrial technologies which are far less costly than they were formerly: all this should bring great benefits to mankind. Unfortunately, this progress has not just opened up new possibilities for peaceful development but also the exact opposite as well. So we must continue to work unceasingly on ways to perfect global security systems in pace with the technical developments which may facilitate them. Unremitting control of dangerous materials and technologies is the key to prevent their proliferation and to provide the foundation of any security system. The most effective means of curbing aggressive ambitions is preventing such proliferation of armaments in general and individual systems on a massive and global scale. Contemporary global civilization has developed an artificial culture dominated by technology, which we ourselves have created and are constantly propagating.

Data provided by the UN show that among all kinds of natural calamities those which are technologically based are third in the number of associated fatalities. Technical progress inevitably heightens the risk of such catastrophes, in that they tend to be caused, at least in part, by the 'human factor' involving stupidity, carelessness or cupidity. Among all the various types of natural disaster the most serious in terms of human fatalities are those involving inundations such as floods and tsunamis, while the second are geological in nature, such as earthquakes, mudflows and volcanic eruptions. The twentieth century has inflicted new threats and risks on the human race, but has at the same time also revealed some new ways of counteracting them. Of these the most significant is undoubtedly that of ensuring stable development. The International Commission on Environmental Protection and Development has defined this as the route of social, economic and political progress, which makes it possible to 'satisfy the needs of the present without undermining the capacities of future generations to satisfy their own requirements'. This concept was exhaustively developed at the UN Conference on the Environment and Development which was held in Rio de Janeiro in 1992.

Unfortunately, mankind is in no position to give up many forms of harmful technology straight away. For that reason much academic, expert and political effort is being put into reassuring the public about making existing technologies safer and more reliable, and finding ways of insuring against the risks which we are obliged to face up to. One way of deflecting the risks is to evolve effective countermeasures, especially when they are known to be more likely to arise from the use of new types of technological processes. This in turn will call for various innovatory programmes on a global and national scale, with pilot projects and vetting procedures designed to show up both the positive and negative characteristics of particular technologies. Where there is a lack of certainty or inadequate scientific evidence about the safety or otherwise of a technology which may carry social or environmental risks, the principle to follow should be the precautionary one of not employing any such technology in the first place. If the technology involves aspects of the style and management required by the project and the way it is organized, this should be gone into carefully before it is adopted, to ensure that it can be effectively operated, with additional quality checks on the product and the processes involved, as well as methods for dealing with possible risks that may arise. The responsibility of the state in such cases must be to create the conditions for a proper interaction between the two processes: of human development on the one hand and technological progress on the other.

DEVELOPMENT OF INFORMATION SYSTEMS AND TECHNOLOGICAL INFRASTRUCTURE

The infrastructure adopted for new technologies must take full account of the importance of human development. When such technologies are introduced they should be made accessible to as wide a circle of the population as possible, they should be quick and flexible in use and universally applicable. Access to technological benefits and the ability to make use of them can, strangely enough, be a mark of separation and division between different social groups and countries.

Many regions which are technologically isolated, particularly in South East Asia and Africa, are also poverty-stricken. In consequence their biggest problems are tropical diseases, low agricultural productivity and environmental degradation, which can only be tackled with the help of present-day technologies. But their poor economic circumstances deny them the necessary access to them: they have no resources to obtain them, nor access to scientific research and the means to exploit it. For poor countries in Africa, especially, disease and tropical infections are a catastrophe which affects everyone and makes overall development extremely difficult. Foreign investors find all of this a great disincentive and the high incidence of diseases is a particular threat to countries which are technologically isolated. Another factor is the increasing divide between developed countries and the rest of the world in the development and use of information technologies. Inequalities between different countries, where the most advanced leave others far behind because of their access to the internet and other information products and services, has come to be known in current literature by the name of the 'Digital Divide'. Thus a number of countries and social groups gain access to high quality information services and products because of their education levels and the development of the technical means to do so. The 'Digital Divide' enables particular countries or particular sectors of the population to use, adapt, generate and disseminate particular forms of knowledge. It operates within individual countries, and between different sectors of the population: the rich and poor, young and old, the healthy and the infirm, and in some countries affects people from ethnic minorities and women.

These technological changes have the effect of making the divide between the prosperous national elites and certain groups in society who were already deprived even greater than it was before. And for the former, particularly in OECD countries, the share of prosperity steadily increases. Statistics show that practically all the new technologies are being created in countries which are home to no more than 15% of the world's population while technical know-how reaches no more than one half of the world's population.

3.5 Strategies for a technological dynamic in world communities

INERTIA AS A STRATEGY

The main trends at work in our present state of development (the sixth technological stage) seem to threaten us with a period of long-term inertia and slower rates of growth in global GNP, primarily as a result of the drop in world prices for oil and other raw materials. This may well lead to a failure to refresh obsolete capital resources, and to a lowering of competitiveness in productive capacity not only in domestic markets, but in foreign ones as well, which would then lead to the economy as a whole lagging behind. One of the conditions underlying such inertia in these circumstances may be that so far there is no model which has won a broad measure of acceptance at home or internationally for a comprehensive post-industrial economic policy. Some economists have taken the view that post-industrial economies do already exist in the developed countries of North America and Western Europe, while the countries of Eurasia are likely to remain in the second tier or be dismissed as hopelessly backward countries still awaiting modernization. Other economists identify post-industrial society with the 'information society' which entails maintaining its technocratic character. In practice, both show present-day technologies in a better light than they are in reality, in justifying a possible scenario for their preservation. My own view is that the choice of an 'inertial' scenario in any form holds out dangers for the future of our societies.

A STRATEGY FOR INNOVATION AND BREAKTHROUGH

The only reliable and realistic scenario for the long-term development of our society is one which involves innovatory breakthrough. Such a strategy is the only possible response to the challenges of the twenty-first century, the economic demands of globalization and the best way of tackling the critical situation which has arisen from the present world recession. The alternative to the world economic recession and the slowdown in productive growth can only be the establishment of a post-industrial form of production of the fifth and sixth technological stages; the transition will of course require radical renewal of the productive mechanisms together with considerable investment in innovation. Some features of the sixth stage level have appeared in developed countries over the past ten years. This has come about mainly as a result of more rapid development of nanotechnology, the new forms of alternative energy, such as that from hydrogen and second-generation biofuels, and the much greater attention now being paid to renewable energy sources.

One might mention also other aspects of the technological revolution which should permit, by the middle of the twenty-first century a transformation of the entire basis on which society rests, to speed up the growth of labour productivity, create the conditions for accelerated economic growth and make available enough resources to raise the level and quality of living standards.

The innovation and breakthrough strategy has as its departure point the concept that with the transition to a knowledge-based society and the establishment of a post-industrial scientific paradigm, it becomes possible to bring together all favourable factors, overcome more quickly the contradictions and dangers of the period of crisis; and embark on the best possible trajectory towards macroeconomic dynamism, while taking account of the inherent constraints, especially environmental and demographic. One might view this scenario as moderately optimistic. Nonetheless, there are certain obstacles in the way.

The first is the fact that there is an accumulation of outdated technologies in the world which are being imported, with some modifications, into the Eurasian community of nations, including into Kazakhstan. This entails a flow of what might be called pseudo-innovations which are based on improved technologies, but already basically outmoded. This hampers the adoption of a fully-fledged innovation and breakthrough scenario for economic development, and has the effect of slowing down the rate of productivity in the country. To overcome this critical situation it will be necessary to increase the volume of investment and introduce more innovation into the economy and its share of GNP, and to reassign investment to research and development, including the innovations of the fifth and sixth technological stages.

Secondly, the critical situation as regards technological development in more backward societies can be seen in the irrational structure of their economies and the capacities they have for innovation and technological development: their orientation is that of earlier industrial societies, including greater exploitation of nature and its resources. The solution here must be found by means of structural reform, including investment in innovation with an increased share of GNP, and concentration on innovative development of human capital and technologies designed to conserve natural resources.

In the third place, the technological gap between leading countries and the majority of the less developed countries is increasing. This reinforces the trend towards lower productivity in the more backward economies and the growing gulf between prosperity and poverty. The global economic crisis at the start of the twenty-first century will reinforce the gap, because the poorer countries possess very little of their own scientific, personnel or investment resources to absorb the new technologies. The only possible solution is a partnership between the leading and less developed societies so as to bring their levels of economic and social development closer together.

In the fourth place, a serious brake on the introduction of innovation into the economies concerned is the severe lack of trained personnel capable of developing, absorbing and exploiting the new technologies. We are speaking here of personnel at all levels of the technological process: scientists, construction workers, engineers, technicians, skilled workers, managers and state administrators.

The main point here is not one of numbers but of the level of professional qualifications and the ability to incorporate radical innovations into the work. This may carry risks, but can also be very successful if personnel can effectively introduce such innovations and find market applications for them. To meet the new challenges of the twenty-first century, industry will need post-industrial methods of production with a high level of starting capital and employment of the latest technology on a large scale. Well-trained workers will be necessary who are also keen to see the introduction of innovative methods and can do so as part of an alliance between the state, business and the scientific and educational communities. International tie-ups will also be needed, to bring a strong flow of new technologies from leading economies to the less developed. This process of adaptation to conditions in more backward economies will, however, demand special conditions to be satisfied.

In the first place, each of the recipient countries will have to develop its own capabilities in applied science and construction, with qualified researchers, builders, planners, engineers, skilled workers and managers. Kazakhstan, as one of the countries of the Eurasian community, is well placed in this respect. We have quite a sound scientific base already and a well-educated workforce which should allow us to go beyond borrowing foreign technology to become technological leaders in our own right. To achieve this we shall need to pursue sound macroeconomic policies with the emphasis on innovation. State investment on a much greater scale, together with resources from private businesses, will also be required if we are to build up our own scientific and technical base without the need, as at present, for such inputs to be borrowed from abroad.

Secondly, Kazakhstan must create the conditions for the employment of the technologies appropriate to the fifth and sixth stages, as already discussed; it is only by these means that we can help to overcome the wider crises we all face in food supplies, energy and the environment, not to mention education and the development of human capital more generally.

In the third place, innovation will not be possible without reform of our investment structures and more capital resources for the adoption of more sophisticated technologies; to succeed with fast-growing new technologies we also have to accept that in the early stages they can carry high risks and need a considerable time to recover their original costs. This is why the state must provide support particularly in the start-up phase, when new generations of technology are just being introduced. Investment will be required for the kinds of technology characteristic of the 'sixth stage', and for the associated staff training, including information technologies and exploitation of the internet. Other crucial factors are resource conservation, adoption of clean manufacturing and planning for innovative technologies at the national level.

In Kazakhstan we are currently developing our capacities for sixth-stage adoption of technology. The crisis of 2007–2009 taught us that it is no use trying to catch up with the global leaders. We will, however, benefit from drawing on their experience to move in their direction, while making use of what we have from our economic development in stages three, four and five in order to move to the sixth stage. This will entail intensive concentration on nanotechnologies, renewable and alternative sources of energy, bionics and similar disciplines.

It will not be enough to define development scenarios a long way ahead. The goal must be an optimistic strategy for innovation and a pioneering effort which we can pursue in a partnership between the state, the business community and within our society more broadly. Success will also depend on structural modernization, to allow the development of manufacturing with a basis in the latest technology which can overcome the gap between ourselves and the scientific and technological leaders. We cannot, for the time being, expect our own innovations to emerge on a massive scale sufficient to create a high technology sector. We must, therefore, gear up for it with work on nanotechnology, biotechnology and information technology. This relates in the first instance to concentration on materials and technical development, with modern communications and infrastructure, and on intellectual development which embraces education, the sciences and a sound research base. Thus, a strategy for technological breakthrough must be based on innovative approaches which can be transferred from the leading economies to those which are less developed and tending to lag behind.

CHAPTER 4

A strategy for radical economic renewal

Economic development in human societies is expressed in a multitude of ways which occur over time in the physical space that different societies actually occupy. It varies greatly in scale and extent, and encompasses powerful economic systems or a number of them; these are identifiable as the big economic systems which major global societies represent. By studying the dynamics of each of these we can arrive at a picture of their cyclical nature, with cycles periodically being replaced by new ones, and society itself being transformed as a consequence. Crises, economic or otherwise, seem to be an inseparable part of this process, and they may be longer or shorter, or more or less far-reaching, depending on the processes which have given rise to them.

4.1 Lessons to be drawn from the current financial and economic crisis

A point of departure can be found in the varied influences a crisis has had on the transformation of the existing economic and other structures, where the conflicting elements include those which have had destructive effects, undermining old practices while hindering further advances, and those whose effects are constructive, and extend the possibilities for introducing new and progressive changes.

CYCLICAL PROCESSES IN ECONOMIC DEVELOPMENT
In the second half of the twentieth century booming economic activity facilitated impressive technical, technological and economic

achievements. In this dynamic atmosphere scientific progress flourished, as did educational and cultural progress across the globe. At the height of the industrial and economic cycle gross domestic product (GDP) achieved its fastest ever rate of growth. In the period 1950 to 1973 this amounted to a yearly increase of 4.9%, and a figure of 2.9% per head of population. In the subsequent decade the equivalent figures saw a reduction to 3.1% and 1.4% and in the 1990s GDP growth was 2.6%.

In the period of transition to the post-industrial phase the factors which contributed to it are difficult to evaluate one way or the other, since as they emerge they display negative as well as positive elements. For instance, greater global influences on the evolution of economic processes can have positive effects if technical and technological advances into higher levels of economic development bring new qualities to them and make them very widely available. Negative influences, by contrast, may become apparent when over-elaborate mechanisms lead to polarization and contradictory influences affect different areas of social, economic or political activity. The key issue is this: how to define and evaluate the factors which contribute to global development; and this must address the best ways of distributing and exploiting and exploit the accumulated resources we have at our disposal.

The neoliberal economic model we use at present was designed to benefit the transnational corporations and the world's richest countries, and has the effect of making the negative aspects of structural changes occurring in the world economy stronger and more extreme. The most developed societies are actually taking over the potential for qualitative change in the new stages of technological development, pushing them in directions which do not always favour the basic transformations needed; sometimes, indeed they can deflect them or postpone them to an indefinite future.

There is plenty of evidence to show that large-scale economic systems at times fail to concentrate their maximum efforts on tackling global economic problems when these involve reducing the gap between rich and poor or developed and developing societies. Their main aim, on the contrary, is to concentrate their capital resources in the countries of the 'golden billion' so that they can gain control of financial income to be derived from them. Evidence for this is provided by market capitalization indicators which, according to the World Bank, amounted to USD43.6 trillion in 2006, which constituted 99% of world GDP, and is largely concentrated in the economies of the developed world. From the end of the twentieth century, and more specifically its last quarter, the global system began to sink into decline, and thence into a state of complete crisis. It seems likely that, even in the event of more favourable circumstances, this will persist throughout the first quarter of the twenty-first century. Conversely, it may be turn out to be more protracted and take up the first half of the century. This stage of global development may thus become a succession of exceptionally long cycles which will result in a profound qualitative renewal.

INTERDEPENDENCE OF TECHNOLOGICAL AND ECONOMIC CYCLES IN A GLOBAL DYNAMIC

The current stage in the balance of economic forces is unique, in that it is defined by crises through which we must pass in the long term, the very long term or as part of millennial cycles. These make it possible to forecast how future economic crises may arise, and to some extent to work out less painful ways of surmounting negative phases, to some degree to compress their timeframes, and to limit their extent within foreseeable limits. In present circumstances, global development, which is by its nature generally cyclical, is now coinciding with the decline of the fifth technological stage through which the developed world has been passing. This is unquestionably the time to prepare for the transition to the next level, the sixth. However, despite its transitory nature, which makes it difficult to define, the instability of our present period quite often exacerbates the overall situation and leads to economic crises which affect all existing communities throughout the world. Consequently, for the time being any negative elements may spread out to the point where they become irreversible.

We can see this in the present financial and economic crisis: though it originated in one particular country, it extended beyond the limits of the financial manipulations in one particular private operation, and acquired the huge dimensions of a process with global dimensions. And no matter how long it may continue, its fall-out will be felt for a long time on global, regional and national economies, and particularly on those countries which are averagely or poorly developed.

What needs to be noted here is that developed economic systems have a habit of unloading the negative consequences of their actions on all members of the global economic community and in particular on those who belong to the weakest and most vulnerable sections of it. Thus, while developed societies and individual countries have at their disposal considerable resources to see them through the impact of major crises, others with far fewer ways of protecting their economies from collapse are the very ones who have to bear the brunt when disaster strikes. The concentration of capital in developed economic systems and the manifest lack of resources in the developing ones hold back and limit the ability of the latter to adopt on a large scale the key technical innovations which would allow them to make the transition to a level compatible with the sixth generation technology.

Again, the objective of those whose possession of major investments makes them rich is to obtain dividends from their capital in the relatively untroublesome virtual sectors of the economy such as financial instruments. They direct considerable streams of investment not into real capital development which might bring about qualitative transformation in the economy, but rather into expanding their virtual financial relationships and speculative operations. Operations of this kind enable investors to acquire substantial profits not derived from real results. Financial capital increases to an enormous extent, far exceeding the capital in the real sectors of the economy and the products created by it.

All this undermines the foundations of balance and stability: it distorts established relationships between different economic systems and provokes destructive changes by causing growing inflation and chaotic price fluctuations. This has negative consequences for all economic relationships. Another consequence is capital flight which weakens already precarious economies to the benefit of stronger ones, with resources going to the creation of virtual capital. Financial flows bypass the real economy, which provides the real reserves needed for promising innovations. This kind of transformation brings about chaotic and negative fluctuations which then become impossible to control. An awareness of the processes at work in the system as a whole at least makes it possible to understand these transformations, so as to avoid their destructive implications and prevent the squandering of the resources which have been built up within the global community.

SUBJECTIVE CAUSES OF THE CURRENT FINANCIAL CRISIS

By analysing the nature of the economic processes at work in contemporary societies we can see how the global economic and financial crisis of 2007–2009 came about as a result of objective causes and laws which apply to economic conditions everywhere. There were also subjective factors at work, and these can be understood not just by the fact that industrial-growth factors had been exhausted and that a new type of economic policy was required with new and more sophisticated underpinnings. The situation requires a refined business methodology which can be described as entailing 'smart' methodology which to a great extent is based on 'virtual' market mechanisms. The economic crisis derived to a considerable extent from the fact that by far the most important factors at work were the operations of the financial institutions and the virtual products for which they were responsible, rather than the real productive sector. Behind this lay the headlong growth of the virtual sector, which converted itself from being a banking intermediary into the creator of structured financial instruments which they then sold on.

In recent years, for example, levels of indebtedness increased rapidly and with them increased risks to the whole financial system. Such changes coincided with the creation of excessive liquidity, and the availability of easy credit increased unproductive demand for financial credits along with increases in their value, which in itself is enough to heighten risk factors. Some economists have likened the situation to the bursting of a debt bubble. Since this debt grew to the size of the world economy, what we got has been a bubble of global dimensions. After evolving in the recesses of the virtual economy, the present financial and economic crisis has acquired the character of a global process which embraces the whole of the world economy, and in this the likely consequences will evidently affect the weak links in the market chain with far greater impact. The global community as a whole, and individual states which form part of it, is taking a large number of consistent initiatives to restrain the scale and extent of the current financial and economic crisis and to speed up a solution to it. I have myself proposed a plan for a radical overhaul of the world's financial system which can be found in my article 'Keys to the Crisis'.[8] I do not believe that this article has lost any of its relevance, and have therefore presented its basic ideas in this present work.

4.2 Keys to the crisis

The world crisis which has recently shaken countries and continents is a phenomenon on a scale which mankind has not previously experienced. It is certainly one of those events which has no analogue in our previous history and it has profoundly changed the world order and its economic foundations. If it is to be properly analysed, thought through and overcome, it will need an imaginative and sceptical approach to all established dogmas and stereotypes. It will not help to look for extremists or for guilty parties. It is more important to identify the defects at the heart of the system which have provoked such powerful upheavals, and most of all to discover how best to eliminate them altogether. We must be bold enough to accept that we are about to create a radically new and differently structured model for the economy, for politics and for global security. We have no alternative if we are truly determined to seize this unique opportunity to overcome the imperfections of the old world and build a new one. This will obviously require colossal efforts from world society as a whole, the mobilization of intellectual and material resources and a great deal of time. We shall have to devise a radical new logic and new 'rules of the road' for the journey which we could provisionally describe as the world of the great transition. The first task is to identify, if we can, the starting principles and origins of this global crisis.

A PROFOUND GLOBAL DEFECT

A century and a half ago, one of our great Eurasian thinkers said that 'Strength without is the fruit of strength within'. This could be confidently paraphrased as 'Crisis without is the fruit of crisis within.' Indeed, our present global crisis is neither some kind of natural calamity nor the result of some accidental combination of circumstances, but the inevitable objective consequence of a profound internal defect. If we fail to define it precisely, any efforts we may make to repair the global monetary and financial system from which the crisis sprang will be no more than purely cosmetic. And in this case the defect, if not dealt with, will give rise to new crises in the future which can be expected to recur with growing frequency and with more grievous consequences. Thus, it came about that our whole world somehow found its way, unexpected and unnoticed, into the tunnel of global crisis, and today hardly anyone can see an exit sign. That probably happened because we are still looking at today's world and at the new world which faces us from the same perspective as we did before. But a radical renewal will demand a renewal of our ways of thinking as well. This will apply to all concepts, categories, theories and ideas, as well as the language we use to describe facts and phenomena in the new world. What is the basis of world development? The core and motive force is the global capital which is what creates the world's prosperity. And what is the basis of capital? The system of global currencies. And finally what is the basis of global currencies? The mechanism for generation and exchange: laws, procedures, emitters, channels, users and so on.

SEVEN SIMPLE QUESTIONS

We could begin the radical review of our thinking with honest answers to the following seven simple questions, which explain in down-to-earth terms what the essence of returning to a healthy monetary system would entail:

1)   Is the present *de facto* global monetary system legal *de jure*?

It seems clear the question of such legality could not arise unless there were established laws on a global currency which had been approved by the heads of a majority of governments and ratified by a majority of the world's parliaments. It would be more exact to describe the existing global monetary system as 'prelegal' in the sense that it appeared *de facto* before the establishment of a global system which could define it as legal *de jure*. For this reason the currency of what we might call the 'New World' can only derive from a 'Global Law' which establishes it, duly signed by a majority of heads of government and approved by their legislatures. The currency could not be that of an already existing state. The Law would have to lay down unequivocally that it had a supranational and intergovernmental status, with the principles of its issuance established by a specially established global Issuance Authority.

A system of this kind could bring into being the first completely legal world currency.

2) Are the procedures employed by the issuing authorities of the world currency really democratically decided?

It is quite clear that it would not be acceptable to give the authorities of only one particular nation the power to take decisions or act as issuer of the world currency. All the operators and users of the new currency should create democratic management mechanisms for those responsible for issuing it, in accordance with its founding law, and employ strictly democratic procedures within the managing administration.

3) Are the mechanisms for balancing the currency's supply and demand competitive and free?

A world market in the global currency could obviously not be competitive and would have to be recognised as such before global institutions were created to establish and control the rules for competitive activities by all those concerned. Such necessary competitive activity could be guaranteed and strictly controlled by a special supervisory body such as a World Antimonopoly Currency Committee. The existing world currency market clearly does not guarantee equal rights to all possible issuing authorities. In the free market it is well known that any privileges for sellers' groups are categorically ruled out, as are open and private limitations on purchasing power and commodity exchange functions for a currency which is being launched on a global level. This is not what we see in this case and the market is clearly not free. A world currency market could be legally supervised by what we might provisionally call a World Free Market Committee. Such an absolutely free market would have to exclude any privileges for any issuers' groups or sellers of the world currency.

4) Can the world currency market be described as civilized?

In a civilized market the rules of play are established and observed on the basis of an agreement between all participants (sellers and buyers) which do not infringe any private interests. In the present world currency market nothing of this kind can, of course, be observed. For the present, the world currency market can consequently not be regarded as civilized. Once the new currency market is functioning, its rules would have to be made legally binding on the basis of a general agreement between all the participants.

5) Will the system for generating and issuing the world currency be under the control of its subjects and users (countries, companies and private citizens) and world society as a whole?

No, none of these will exercise such control. In that sense the issuance system is absolutely uncontrolled. All the principal subjects and users (countries, companies and private citizens) must have the right to create permanently valid mechanisms for controlling its generation, issue and circulation, as envisaged by the law in question. The activities of the issuer must also be kept under the control of all three branches of power, the legislative, the executive and the judiciary.

6) Is the system for generating and issuing the world currency answerable to its subjects and users (countries, companies and private citizens) and world society as a whole?

The issuers of world currency have had no such responsibility to any of the individuals or bodies named, including world society as a whole. In that sense the issuers have been without any responsibility, which is what provoked the global crisis. All legitimate and lawful issuers must bear full responsibility for their actions – or inaction – to its subjects and users and this could be legally guaranteed by, for example, a World Currency Arbitrator.

7) Is the world currency system effective in the sense that its results correspond to the development goals of the world community as a whole?

In practice, the functioning of the world currency system led to a situation in which the very existence of a flourishing global capital market and stable global development (like a single world currency) are at present under threat. This is evidence enough of its complete ineffectiveness. The issuing authorities must fully satisfy the key objectives and values of mankind and world society, just as the practical results of the new currency system must fully meet the aims and tasks required for stable development and prosperity. These principles need to be laid down in law as a basis for the whole system governing the new currency, along with a system for regular monitoring and adjustment.

If honest answers are given to these seven simple questions they will make the question of whether the current financial arrangements are adequate to the challenges of the new century entirely rhetorical.

Since the middle of the last century our world has undergone radical changes, and at a speed which increases with every passing day. The only thing which does not change is the essence of the mechanism for generating and circulating currency that has been used throughout the world, and the pace at which it is being brought up to date lags catastrophically behind the changes occurring in the world. That is to say that the world currency system has long since become obsolete, and irreversibly so, which only goes to confirm the extent of the global crisis. The whole mechanism of the new currency system should be built on a special system of precautionary monitoring for the approaching challenges of the age, the world and mankind, drawing on the seven principles noted above. Only in this way can a new world currency system keep up to date, and be a productive source, without built-in defects, not of global crises, but of steady development worldwide and in a flourishing human society.

FROM WHERE, AND TO WHERE ARE WE GOING?

To begin with, let us remember that up to now the driving force behind the Old World was global capital, which was built on a global currency which was inherently deeply flawed. This Old World is often associated with the expression 'world capitalism', though we already understand that capital which operates with a defective currency would be better and more honestly referred to by a more accurate name, like 'defective capital'. Not long ago, hundreds of billionaires all over the world experienced for themselves how defective their illusory capital was when literally over a period of several months almost all of it suddenly disappeared. The force driving the New World will have to be some form of radically new capital. To put it more precisely, wealth will have to be self-sustaining and based on a radically new form of currency which will need a new and more adequate description. The ancient Greeks used the beautiful word 'acme' to describe the highest level of development, and our successors will some day have to choose a name for this new and faultless 'more than capital'. It follows that the name of the new currency might well incorporate this word as a prefix and thus be called 'acme capital'; while the structure of the New World, with 'acme capital' as its radically new driving force, would not longer be capitalism, but what might now be called 'acme capitalism'. A somewhat unconventional approach such as this, with a new name for a new era of development, should enable us to prepare all the more effectively for it, with a deeper understanding of the true nature of our new, renewed world. And what is most important, it should give us new practical tools to guide us in our new journey towards the New World, to see it for what it is, and have the confidence to operate within it.

TRANSITION TO THE FUTURE

A key concept in understanding the nature of the stage of growth reached by the new world we are now approaching is what we might describe as a period of 'transit'. And the new kind of transitional prosperity would based on the employment of a world currency whose operations had as yet been only partially perfected; it would be right to define this as 'transitional capital' rather than 'acme capital'. Correspondingly, the time period in which the transit takes place would be defined not as 'acme capitalism' but as 'transitional capitalism', albeit with a worldwide financial infrastructure of a new kind and quality. The main task and mission of this transitional stage would be to prepare for the transition from the old flawed currency to the new and perfected world system employing the 'acme currency'. This would entail removing, or at least redistributing, the burdens on the world system with the old flawed currency system to a new arrangement of regional and continental issuance centres with currency and accounting units set up at the level of regions and supranational and intergovernmental bodies. As for the legal system, this would function at regional and continental levels as it does throughout the world. Just as no one national currency can effectively function at the global level, no regional currency could be expected to function as effectively as a centrally issued supranational and intergovernmental one.

As far back as the year 2003, Kazakhstan proposed that the Eurasian Economic Association should introduce such a supranational unit for its own use, with the suggested name of the 'altyn'. For several years now detailed work has gone into the creation of regional and supranational currencies. What one might call the 'first swallow' was the European Currency Unit, the ECU, which with the passage of time was transformed into the fully fledged European supranational currency, the Euro. Similar processes are in train with the Asian Currency Unit, in the Persian Gulf region, with what is variously called the Dinar, Khaleeji or Djouman, and in Latin America, where the Alba organization has an accounting unit known as the 'Sucre', from the Spanish 'Sistema Unitario de Compensacion Regional'. Similar initiatives are being taken in Africa, where preparations have been going on for some time for the introduction of a currency to the called the 'Afro'.

By their nature, all these regional initiatives for currency integration are important landmarks in the development of regional centres of 'transitional capital' throughout the world. It is worth noting that preparations for the introduction of regional supranational accounting units began in various regions of the world long before the global financial crisis began. Indeed, this started the process of developing regional and continental centres of 'transitional capital' with regional issuing centres for supranational 'transit' currencies. That is to say that the world was already preparing spontaneously for the next stage of renewal through the formation of regional centres for the issue of supranational currency long before the start of the global crisis.

CAPITAL NOAH'S ARK

Those whose economic interests are tied up with the old order, with its faulty capital structure, can quickly grasp their predicament if they look at it from the following extreme perspective: the whole world as we know it today is slowly but surely sinking into the morass created by our global crisis. And 'transitional capital' is a special kind of 'Capital Noah's Ark' which can save our assets from the flood created by the global crisis. For this reason it would be wise for anyone concerned about their assets to convert them as soon as possible.

It is only this, the Capital Noah's Ark, which can rescue these assets and transfer them completely into the refuge provided by the New World. Kazakhstan and its partners in regional and continental integration, the Commonwealth of Independent States (CIS), the Eurasian Economic Association (EAEA), the Central Asian Union (CAU) and the Shanghai Cooperation Organisation

(SCO), have been closely involved in the global movement of the first quarter of the twenty-first century which seeks to set up organizations to promote regional integration. All those just mentioned, albeit with different stages of preparedness, have the capacity to become regional transcapital areas with their own issuing centres for intergovernmental and supranational accounting/currency units. Kazakhstan is ready to proceed step by step, in partnership with the EAEA and SCO, to create favourable conditions for the establishment of an issuing centre for the new Eurasian supranational accounting unit, which could be known by its initials, ENRE in Russian or ESAU in English.

Given the special and unique composition of its issuing authorities (the countries of the EAEA and the SCO, and neighbouring India and Pakistan) the ESAU could simultaneously be brought into a close and organic relationship both with the European zone of the euro and of other regional zones with supranational accounting units. The region enjoys an exceptionally advantageous position from a geographical standpoint, and if the interests of regional and continental holders of 'transit capital' were duly taken into account, this position could give it a unique opportunity to build on the ESAU to create a new intercontinental transit currency, bringing the world 'acme currency' a step closer.

Even this transitional stage will clearly be insufficient in our present state of global crisis. For this reason the establishment of the regional and continental transit centre network (to assume responsibility for the defective system constituted by the old world currency) needs to be accompanied by preparations, in parallel, for the transition to the new unflawed system of the new global 'acme currency'; this will, in turn, become the heart of the forthcoming era of 'acme capital'.

PLAN FOR RADICAL RENEWAL (PRR)
Our period of global 'transit' does not have all that much time or resources to prepare for this historic transition. The time for

starting the design and construction of the new 'Capital Noah's Ark' is actually already behind us. The world's leaders, therefore, need to start this very day on their preparations for a practical transition to global 'acme capitalism'; if they fail to do so, the issues of stable development and prosperity may well need to be put off for decades to come. The project must be put on the agenda of all the major political and economic organizations, summits and world forums: the UN Security Council, the UN special session, the G8, the G20, the world economic forum in Davos, and so forth.

A precise plan for radical renewal must be the first practical step, and it could use all the arguments already adduced in this study as a foundation. It should be understood that no bodies, organizations or summits can achieve productive and effective results unless they work out and act upon plans for radical renewal; furthermore, this renewal, this transition from the old world order to a new one must become the global trend in the first quarter of the twenty-first century. Whatever the level of the renewal, whether by region or globally, it will not produce the right results unless it incorporates key elements for the transition from the old and defective currency system to the new stable transitional one, whether at the global or regional level. It will need also the technical means for converting the old unstable currency to the new system of 'transit capital' and for setting up regional issuing centres which can handle it. The renewal plan must also be able to assist political and social bodies at all levels in facilitating their countries' and peoples' transition from the old defective capital arrangements to the new. The radically new approaches outlined above to analysis, understanding and practical renewal at a time of global crisis may be the only basis for discussion and resolution of such a wide range of issues in a single comprehensive system.

To these conceptual contributions Kazakhstan can also add other very varied organizational solutions to the problems involved. We are ready to make arrangements for international forums to be held at the highest level to coordinate the work of regional and continental centres involved with the operations of 'transit capital'. We can work together to research and plan global and applied scenarios to bring to successful and rapid conclusion the 'transitional capital' stage we have now reached, and then the practical steps required for transition to the next stage of 'acme capitalism'. The EAEA and the SCO, as founders of the Eurasian transit centre, could also launch an accelerated release of transit currency, not only in Eurasia and other continents but also on a global basis. The countries of the EAEA, and perhaps the SCO countries, could also coordinate their efforts to promote such a global initiative in international and world bodies, organizations and forums. It is interesting to note that at the beginning of January, 2009, the leaders of the European Union held a summit in Paris, 'New World, New Capitalism', at which they discussed similar problems, though under somewhat different headings. We should consider the possibilities of organising a global discussion of the Plan for Radical Renewal in a three-sided meeting with the EAEA, the SCO and the European Union. To judge from the topics discussed in Paris and in similar forums elsewhere, all of us in different continents are speaking with one voice about the same problems.

THE UNIQUE EXPERIENCE OF RENEWAL

With each month and day the growing global crisis presents us with unique and astonishing opportunities for renewal, but with less and less time to take advantage of the rare chances we are offered. There has never been a previous period when our world had such unlikely opportunities for self-renewal and practical ways of realising the future we wish for. When considering the ways in which regional groupings can help us integrate our efforts to overcome the global crisis we cannot of course relieve our national governments of responsibility for playing an effective part in the process. The members of the CIS have accumulated exceptional experience over the past two decades in economic renewal, to an extent other states cannot match. They must now make full use of their former expertise in crisis management. Kazakhstan shares with all new independent states the experience of more than once having to overcome very difficult times. After the collapse of the Soviet Union we experienced the torments of renewal and lived through complex and arduous periods of reform. We succeeded in what seemed like insurmountable challenges, and won. There is no reason why we should not do so again: we now have more resources and greater possibilities than before.

More than ten years ago we began to put together a special National Reserve Fund by putting aside substantial income from raw material exports. The purpose was to expand our human dimension, to save for future generations and to take stabilization measures in case of crises. At the present time the Fund is working at full stretch, so that we can support a dynamic programme of basic economic and social programmes. Quite obviously it would be extremely difficult to cope with current global problems on our own, and perhaps even impossible. That is why we are strong supporters of integration at the global as well as the regional level. This is one of our highest priorities in combating the crises we face. It is precisely for that reason that we are working on a practical initiative to work for renewal on a global, regional and all other levels. This should make it quicker and more effective to get work through the period of transition, and move on to preparations for the new world of 'acme capitalism' which is what human society really needs, whatever name it eventually is given.

WHO WILL BENEFIT?

On the basis of this initiative, the Plan for Radical Renewal (PRR), the United Nations could start work on the revision and redrafting of the Agenda for the third millennium. This is essential for a truly substantive and comprehensive transition from the old order to a radically new one, to be known as 'acme capitalism'. The PRR is crucial as a practical guide to our escape from the current crisis. The planning involved is vital for all those involved in global development, whether countries, transnational corporations or international organisations. The same is true for everyone concerned with the real economy, such as state and private enterprises, firms and organizations which need practical guidance on the principles of transitional capital and the new global transit currency. To give it full effect global bodies will need radical innovation in the sciences and industry and in the fields of finance and currency management as well. The PRR will give them practical means of coordinating work on the infrastructure and operational mechanisms they will need. The PRR can also bring countries and peoples together, unite their efforts on the basis of their shared interests and help them with new mechanisms to build a safer world. The basis for this will be the powerful new financial and economic foundations provided by the sound new world currency.

NEW GLOBAL KEY MARKET FOR THE WORLD

The most powerful and varied organisations and individuals have been trying for the past year and a half at a variety of levels to discover and draw up a wide range of solutions to the ongoing crisis. As a result of their efforts a new and very particular kind of global market has emerged. This has a range of prescriptions and plans designed for this purpose, a kind of market in 'keys' to the crisis. The demand for this has so far greatly exceeded the supply. Two approaches have emerged, a broad one and a narrow one.

The first, the broad one, consists of decisions and prescriptions for a superficial, cosmetic reconstruction of the global currency and financial system. The second, the narrow one, aims for radical cures on a global scale involving the correction of profound genetic defects which have shown up in our global system. The plan we have proposed for radical renewal is indeed the second of these; the PRR is a new commodity from the second narrow sector from the world market in the aforementioned 'keys'. And the Plan for

Radical Renewal is perhaps the first global key to the issue of radical renewal which the world crisis has presented us with. If the emerging world 'transitional capital' is really a 'Capital Noah's Ark', then the PRR we have proposed is a first blueprint for the construction of this new Noah's Ark. And if a Eurasian centre for 'transitional capital' does materialize, it might very well turn out to be the first centre of this life-saving structure. Such an approach would benefit the whole world. We went into the global crisis together, and we should also together be able to turn the global key to it.

4.3 Renewal after the crisis and the development of the Eurasian economic association

Overcoming the negative consequences of the growing global crisis requires short-term measures which will have to be followed by a medium-term programme and then by a long-term strategy to lay down guidelines for the each country's scientific and technological development. The spread of economic recession throughout the world has also obliged many governments to rethink their long-term development strategies. However, the ways in which the economies of individual states, as well as that of the world as a whole, are affected are so many and various that it is well-nigh impossible to define uniform scenarios for the long term with any real confidence. For that reason the best strategic approach must involve careful analysis and comparison of all available theories and economic models. The task is made no easier by the wide divergence of expert views from one country to another. For the Eurasians, and specifically for Kazakhstan and Russia, the choice of scenarios may be somewhat limited. For example, a paper by Russian economists reviews four possible long-term scenarios, as follows: 'superindustrial modernisation', 'the rush to globalisation', 'economic isolationism', and 'energy and selfishness'.

Of these, only the first employs a progressive approach to economic policy, entailing capitalization of comparative advantages in the national economy, and modernization of large-scale production in manufacturing industry. The other scenarios involve only one of the directions laid down and 'energy and selfishness' does not address any of them. The conclusion is that the strategy best suited to the countries of Eurasia is the first of the four.

Another group of Russian economists also suggests a range of scenarios as a means of choosing between alternative strategies. Their choice concentrates on possible long-term approaches summarised as 'The Investor', 'Mobilization', 'Inertia', and 'Modernization'. We can review these briefly in turn. The first means that all efforts and financial resources are concentrated on developing branches of the economy connected with the extraction and export of natural resources; the income derived from this is centralised and redistributed through the state budget only for social expenditure and national defence. This type of development will benefit only those companies which are involved in the extraction and exporting business, such as oil, gas and metals. In practice it means rejection of innovative activity outside the extractive sector, curtailing infrastructure projects, a standstill in production in the manufacturing industries and a growth in the import of goods and services.

Future developments according to this scenario are likely to involve a fall in raw material extractive sectors because of the growing burden of social expenditure and, of course, the depletion of oil and gas reserves. The scenario under 'Mobilization' involves modernization focussed on sectors and regions, where the state supports only those branches and manufacturers which are selected as high priority, which do not involve a dialogue with the business sector and are directed towards existing undertakings. The redistribution of resources from the raw material sector is done either through the budget or through state corporations created on a top-down basis with financial means provided by the state. A scenario of this type takes very little account of the citizen's interests, and development of low priority branches of industry is given only residual support, which leads to their gradual decline. The reallocation of resources to narrowly defined priorities has been shown by experience elsewhere to lead to the partial reallocation of other resources and to a sharp decline in the effectiveness of government expenditure.

The long-term strategy pursued under the 'Inertia' scenario puts stability ahead of development. This involves the continuation of already established trends and leads to technological backwardness: radical economic and institutional changes are avoided and innovation is lacking. The weaknesses of this approach are very clear. Finally, there is the fourth scenario for long-term development under the title of 'Modernization', which envisages a complex of institutional changes designed to create favourable conditions and stimuli for innovative changes in the economy and society. In practice this involves transition to innovative development not through the redistribution of resources by the state, but by creating new resources through innovation and new mechanisms resulting from partnership between the state and the private sector. The last two strategies for long-term development have emerged from studies which address issues of scientific and technological development in the Eurasian community up to the year 2030. There are two variants, out of a number of possible economic scenarios, which have good prospects for successful implementation and offer freedom of choice to social and political forces. They are the inertial and innovatory, described in my last chapter. What I would like to do at this point is describe some of their economic assumptions, factors and possible consequences:

1) The inertial approach which aims to retain, with some modifications, the trends in economic development which emerged at the end of the twentieth century and the beginning of the twenty-first;

2) A scenario for innovative breakthrough which requires not only technological but also economic innovation of a post-industrial type, the formation of an effective many-layered economic structure, gradual removal of polarization in society and positive structural changes in the economy.

Both scenarios have a number of shared features and tendencies:

a) maintaining the general trend towards economic growth, increasing labour productivity and standards of living, though with varying speeds, and to varying degrees, by region and local culture, and with possible reductions at certain times, for example when signs of economic crisis appear;

b) the influence of periodic economic crises is maintained, but with variations in economic parameters, depth, timeframe and consequences arising from them;

c) the trend will continue towards the globalization of productive forces and economic institutions, though in accordance with varied models and varying levels of social and economic disparity;

d) the mutual influence of the various elements in society and the economy will continue. However, in accordance with the innovation and breakthrough scenario, a balance will be maintained between groundbreaking technological, institutional and social innovations and transformations.

According to the inertial scenario, uncertainties and divergences in society will become stronger, along with changes for the worse in institutions and administrative mechanisms, and, as a consequence of this, in various spheres and branches of society which will noticeably diminish their overall effects.

The global financial and economic crisis which emerged against the background of the instabilities in the international political situation demonstrates the complexity of the crisis that has developed in the whole system of global regulation. The currently prevalent currency and financial system no longer satisfies today's requirements and does not correspond either to any of the criteria required for the stability of the world's economy. Global currency arrangements have no legitimacy *de jure*. The mechanisms for balancing supply and demand in the world's currencies are uncompetitive and lacking in freedom. The system for issuing world currency is uncontrollable and is not responsive to the needs of world markets Many countries are now putting forward a variety of models for reform of the system, including Germany, Russia, China, Turkey and countries of the Islamic world.

I myself set out my vision for resolving global problems. I believe, as I have indicated above, that the crucial step will be to create a single global currency under the aegis of the United Nations. The time has come to move over to a completely new regime for a world currency based on a single, global accounting and payments unit which would be legally based and accepted by all the countries of the world. All countries would take part in creating it, issuing it and providing regulatory mechanisms. The transition to the new system would, of course, have to take place gradually.

The present crisis has caused the divergence that has arisen between the real gross production society has created and the virtual capital, derived from speculation, which is not guaranteed by real underlying assets. We have to face up to the fact that the currency and financial system now prevailing is hopelessly divorced from today's world and its needs; indeed, it is only holding everything back. Any productive process depends for its development on keeping the technology on which it relies updated. And radical renewal of any technology depends on a shift in the paradigm which itself depends on epoch-making innovation. That is to say that there are three stages in the renewal of any of the spheres of the economy and society.

According to Thomas Kuhn, these processes of renewal must proceed in step with those occurring in the sciences, technical development and industry, otherwise there will simply be stagnation. The economic foundations on which the contemporary monetary and financial system rests were laid down by Adam Smith and his concept of the 'invisible hand of the market'. And that, as is well known, emerged in the 1770s at around the same time as James Watt's steam engine. Our current monetary and financial system is far removed from the principles underlying present-day global financial and information technologies, and cannot fully satisfy the needs of today's more complex world. In such circumstances it must be obvious that a cosmetic reform of the world's monetary and financial system which does not reach down to the roots of these contradictions will not bring about any clear improvement either. It is obviously convenient to ascribe all the disorders of the economy, the lack of initiative and any sense of responsibility to the 'invisible hand of the market'. But we have reached the point where we really must accept responsibility for our own futures. If we cannot in the very near future bring about a fundamental renewal of our own economic destiny the prospects for mankind's survival must be poor indeed. The global economic crisis has destroyed any idea that western liberalism and the free market are the only ways forward for mankind to follow. There are now new centres of power emerging in the world and their influence will be felt in the way our societies now develop.

The 'End of History' pronounced by Francis Fukuyama has not materialised. On the contrary, what we are seeing is a new historical period in which different models of economic and political development will exist and compete with one another. The current world crisis has shattered many illusions. The main trend which will follow it will be to transform a unipolar into a multipolar world and with it a strengthening of the forces of regionalism. Within these, in turn, we shall see regional markets developing, in which most goods and services will be produced and consumed. In this way groupings will form which will coalesce on a continental scale. There is an increasing tendency, as world development proceeds, for countries to protect their own national interests within a single geographical area. Examples can be found in Latin

America, in the Persian Gulf region and in eastern Asia. A similar process had previously emerged in the 'euro zone'.

I am now more convinced than ever that there is no alternative in the long term to the integration of the Eurasian area. 'Good fortune resembles a tender but feckless mother who spoils her own children,' said Seneca. When external developments seemed so favourable at an earlier stage, people were prone to close their eyes to the factors which were holding back processes leading to closer integration. We no longer have the right to do that. It is only by working together that we can secure stable economic development for our various countries; the principle of partnership which this entails must be put at the very centre of our strategy for radical renewal of our economic life.

Conclusion

The crucial issues that the twenty-first century must address involve interaction between nation states and local societies across the globe, and the transition from the period of confrontation and conflict to a dialogue and partnership based on the interests we all share, namely the need for stable development for all humankind and our global civilization. The many aspects of this problem cover a broad spectrum of issues which can only be addressed through dialogue and partnership. In the present book I have tried to analyse possible paths we might take in resolving the most momentous problems our society is facing:

1) The search for a shared solution to the global energy and environmental crisis which has enveloped us, the destination being a twenty-first-century revolution in which we shall make the transition to a means of production and consumption which uses all the highest resources of mankind and moves towards alternative, ecologically clean sources of energy;

2) Steps to overcome the economic and technological polarization of communities and individual countries, which has

condemned billions of people in developing countries to backwardness and poverty;

3) Partnership in the social and cultural spheres, and in the sciences, education and cultural and religious communities;

4) The establishment of a multipolar world which will be the chief guarantee for preserving stable development in a complex and multifarious global environment, while maintaining a dynamic balance within it.

I have come to the firm conclusion that in the search for effective solutions to these problems global society is well capable of devising strategies for a radical renewal founded in partnerships between all world communities. This we can achieve by relying on the network of global institutions which already exist, such as the UN, the 192 Group, the G8, the G20 and the various international organisms represented by the European Union, the Commonwealth of Independent States, the EAEA, the SCO, the OSCE, the Conference for Cooperation and Trust in Asia and others. Kazakhstan was a founding member of that strategically important regional institution, the Shanghai Cooperation Organisation, which recently celebrated its tenth anniversary. The members of the SCO and its observers make up the overwhelming majority of the world's population and of its GDP, they have a significant proportion of the planet's mineral and other natural resources; and they possess, furthermore, historic experience of development, dialogue and cooperation.

The Conference on Cooperation and Confidence Building in Asia (CCCBA) is a comparatively young and unconventional forum. It is another meeting ground for dialogue and mutual understanding between political leaders of Asian countries, which helps them to find common approaches and solutions to current issues of trade and economic cooperation, to tackle those regions where deprived areas and run-down social conditions persist, and to deal with conflicts, thus facilitating dialogue and understanding between different cultures, religions and societies. It is a structure which could well be used to spearhead the efforts of the United Nations to resolve the problems I have outlined. It could also be transformed into a new organization for security and cooperation in Asia (OSCA), since we now have all the prerequisites for an 'A-20' which unites 90% of the territory of Asia. The task of resolving global problems already exists; this book now offers politicians, cultural leaders and religious figures a way to tackle them by means of a radical renewal of global society through partnership between the world's different communities. I cannot myself see any other way of addressing the complex issues we face.

There have been quite a number of successful partnerships in the past and at present, and the one thing needed now is resolution on the part of the world's communities to bring this radical renewal into being. The aim of this book has been to indicate the milestones which might make it possible to develop a strategy for such radical renewal of global society. They can be used to distinguish a real strategy from the maintenance of social and political illusions.

I trust that the proposals I have made for such a strategy of renewal will prove to be of some value to the global community, as it strives for the stable development of each and every nation and community on our planet.

References:

1. Resolution 56/6 of the UN General Assembly 'Global agenda for a dialogue between Civilizations' (9 November 2001)

2. General Declaration of UNESCO on cultural diversity, 9 November 2001

3. N.N. Moiseyev: *The Fate of Civilization: The Path of Reason*, 1998

4. Global Environment Outlook 4 (GEO-4): Environment for Development, UNEP, 2007

5. 2007 World Development Indicators, Washington 2007, The World Bank, 2007

6. Education for informational societies in the twenty-first century. Summit document of the G8, St Petersburg, 2006

7. V.I. Danilov-Danilyan. Stable development (theoretical and methodological analysis, Vice-President of the Russian Ecological Academy: http://www.opec.ru/analize_doc.asp?d_no=30047

8. N. Nazarbayev: 'Keys to the crisis', Rossiiskaya Gazeta, 2009, No. 4839

Additional sources:

Bridging the Digital Divide: Internet Access in Central and Eastern Europe: http//www.cdt/org/international/ceeaccess/

The energy/ecological future of civilization. Materials for the Second Civilization Forum, Astana 18–21 September 2008

N. Nazarbeyev: *Strategy for the Establishment of a Post-Industrial Society and a Partnership of Civilizations*, Ekonomika, 2008

V.I. Vernadski: *Studies for a General History of Science*, Nauka 1988

N.D. Kondratyev: *Large Scale Market Cycles and the Theory of Foresight*, Ekonomika 2002

REFERENCES

P.A. Sorokin: *Man, Civilization and Society*, Politizdat, 1992

E. Toffler: *The Third Wave*, ACT, 1999

I.A. Schumpeter: *A History of Economic Analysis*, three volumes, 2001

Yu.V. Yakovets: *Epochal Innovation of the Twenty-first Century*, Ekonomika, 2004